Every Good Wish

John MacNally

Ireland's Own John MacNally

A Life in Song

• • •

John MacNally

With Antonia Felix

For any additional information contact:

P.O. Box 5005
Brentwood
TN, 37027
U.S.A.

ISBN: 1-56171-233-7

10 9 8 7 6 5 4 3 2 1

Manufactured in the United States of America

To Anne
(With Love and Thanks)

I have spread my dreams under your feet;
Tread softly
Because you tread on my dreams.

—W.B. Yeats
"The Cloths of Heaven"

Acknowledgments

For their enormous help in digging up photographs, reviews, and other documents, I would like to thank Cheryll Owen, my son Austin and daughter Elizabeth, and my family in Ireland, especially Donal.

Reflection

As I look back at the part of my career reflected in this book, I feel very privileged that I have been able to make a comfortable living doing the one thing that gives me the most pleasure in life; singing. The fact that it brings pleasure to others is even more gratifying. It has brought me to many parts of the world, enabled me to meet a multitude of people, both on and off the stage, and to perform for many different kinds of audiences from Sydney to Toronto, New York to Tokyo, back to Dublin, and many other places.

But I think this time in my career is the most exciting, with many new things happening and indeed about to happen. I look forward to the future with great enthusiasm, anticipation, hopes for unfulfilled ambitions, new goals to be reached, new audiences, and ventures into many new directions. I hope that you, dear reader, will be part of all this excitement, whether it be on record, radio, TV or stage.

J.M.
Nashville, September 1992

Contents

1 Dublin 1

2 Music and Medicine 9

3 The MacNally Clan 19

4 Taking Off "Down Under" 27

5 On the Road in the U.S.A. 37

6 Australia and Beyond 43

7 All Roads Lead to Nashville 55

8 You Can Take the Man Out of Ireland... 61

Discography 67

Chapter One

Dublin

I can't remember a time when I didn't sing. I was born in Dublin, Ireland, the youngest of six children, and although my parents were not professional singers, ours was a very musical family.

Ireland has a long tradition of annual music festivals and competitions called the Féis (pronounced *fesh*). There are several types of Féis , including the John McCormack Trophy, named after the great Irish tenor, the Dramatic Cup for opera, and the Silver Rose Bowl for German Lieder singing. My first participation in a Féis was also my first opportunity to sing in front of people by myself. At age eleven I competed in the Father Mathew Féis, and true to the form of the absolute rascal everyone expected me to be, I made an appearance that is quite memorable.

As we were getting ready to leave for the festival, my mother asked me to dry my just-washed short pants in front of the electric fire. Typically, my mind was wandering. I daydreamed about being outside, as I was much more interested in playing with my friends than going to a singing competition. Suddenly

I smelled something burning, and snatched my shorts from near the fire. A huge scorch mark had ruined the front right leg of the trousers. In my panic-stricken attempt to wipe it off, I proceeded to make a nice, large hole. I didn't dare show my mother, and managed to hide the disaster all the way to the Féis . When my number was announced and I walked onstage to sing, my mother nearly died to see her lovely son parading in front of the crowd with a burnt-out hole in his gray short pants. The only thing that saved me from her wrath was the fact that *I won the Féis !*

We had a lovely home on Fortfield Road in Terenure, a suburban section of Dublin, and I spent my first school years at the nearby Boys School. Family and friends tell me I was a wild child—a real troublemaker—who was constantly getting into some kind of mischief. When I wasn't pushing neighbor's kids off the wall or robbing apples from the local orchard, I was creating some sort of havoc in school or at home, and, being the youngest, I usually got away with it. But in spite of all the pranks, I had plenty of friends in the neighborhood, and was madly in love with Claire Dowling, the little girl who lived two doors down from me.

One of my earliest memories is that of being rushed to the hospital in the doctor's car after swallowing an entire bottle of iron pills. I remember speeding through all the red lights without stopping, but I don't remember anything about the hospital, or why I decided to eat the pills in the first place. When I was a bit older, I nearly lost three fingers after catching my right hand in a cement-block machine on a building site. My mother nearly fainted at the sight of me, covered in blood, walking up to the house with a man from the construction crew. Luckily, a skilled young doctor named Sean Heffernan believed the fingers could be saved, against the judgment of the rest of his staff, and he stitched everything up perfectly. This remarkable doctor came to know and look after the MacNally family for many years, and was my mother's surgeon during the illness late in her life.

Although the Father Mathew Féis was my first experience singing solo in public, the MacNally family sang at home all the time. And as a boy soprano throughout my childhood, I was also an accomplished choir singer. My brother Donal and I earned a couple of shillings every week singing in the John's Lane Choir in Dublin. The shillings usually disappeared into a slot machine in a small shop near the church, but the musical experiences of the choir were to last a lifetime.

When I think back on those days, I realize there is something very special about making music as a child. The pure and simple pleasure of singing a choral piece for the first time, with the openheartedness and fresh enthusiasm that children bring to things, is a pleasure that seems to be reserved for just that time in one's life. There is little that can compare to the feeling of singing side by side with one's friends, day after day, in the glow of beautiful music and sweet voices.

The John's Lane Choir was directed by a wonderful blind organist, Daniel McNulty, who was also one of my singing teachers. He was devoted to his vocation as teacher and organist, and was always very interested in the boys' progress in music. I invited Mr. McNulty to perform with his choir at my Dublin National Concert Hall concert in 1990, and it was a thrill to see him with his choir again.

When I was a lad of eleven I also earned my first professional fee, thanks to a comedian who lived just down the road from us, "Micky" Heron. Michael and his entire family were close friends of the MacNallys', and Mrs. Heron often looked after me when my parents were away. This was great for me (and no doubt exasperating for her), as she had a real talent for making lovely

Irish soda bread and griddle bread. Micky was busy putting together one of his many concerts, this one to be held in the town of Arglass in the north of Ireland, and he asked if I would join him on the program. Still excited from my success at the Féis , I was ecstatic at the thought of taking a trip and actually making a professional appearance. I was lucky to have a good singing voice, because it was the only thing that could make up for all the devilish things I did. Only an angelic-looking choirboy could get away with taking a trip away from home after almost blowing up the science lab at school! My parents were delighted over the opportunity for me to appear with the famous Micky Heron, so I made the trip and sang the concert. When we arrived home the following evening, Micky asked me to open my hand and dropped five shillings into it. As I stared at the two large, shiny half crowns, I asked myself how I would ever live long enough to spend it all.

When I was thirteen I had a short bout of seriousness toward my life, and decided I wanted to be a priest. I entered Redemptorist College in Limerick, Ireland, but soon realized I didn't have the wherewithal for such an important vocation. So I returned to Dublin and entered Synge Street, the school that would provide me with a sound education, in spite of myself. Synge Street is a very famous school whose staff has educated many of Ireland's great entertainers. Run by the Christian Brothers, it's a tough school, and pranks such as mine were met with strict punishments, such as being thrown out of the choir for a term (which I'm sure I deserved for one offense or another).

Sports as well as music were very important at Synge Street, and I especially enjoyed running the 100- and 200-yard dashes. They were my strong points in sprint, but I also did well in the long jump, holding the interschools athletic record for some time. The love of sports I developed at Synge Street continued beyond my school years, with plenty of competition in meets around Dublin. In addition to being avid football and hurling players, my brother Donal and I thoroughly enjoyed going "pot hunting," as the track-and-field meets were called, trying to win as many prizes, or "pots," as we could.

Interrupted only by the fun of outdoor sports, these were days of being completely immersed in music, and enjoying the excitement and energy of being surrounded by friends and fellow students who shared the same passion for it.

As I approached my leaving examinations at Synge Street, I began to take my classical-music training quite seriously. Learning German Lieder, opera arias and Irish ballads was a labor of love under the expert guidance of Father Brendan Lawless—"Benny," as he was known to all of us. One of Terenure's parish curates, Benny was also a gifted pianist. Some of our days would begin at 7:00 *A.M.*, when we would sing until breakfast a couple hours later. Then it was back to the piano until lunchtime, which would give us the energy we needed to sing for several more hours until dinner. The entire evening would be filled with more music-making, often lasting into the early hours of the morning.

After graduating from Synge Street, I entered Dublin's College of Music to study singing with Kathleen Uheleman and Michael O'Higgins. From there I transferred to the Academy of Music, and studied with the renowned baritone and teacher Dennis Noble.

It was during my days at the Academy that I performed in one of the biggest occasions of my career, a gala concert for Monaco's Prince Rainier and Princess Grace during their state visit to Ireland. I knew that I was just a student—not even close to a seasoned professional—so the thought of singing for such a grand occasion made me quite nervous. And to make it even worse, the night before the concert I dreamed that I walked out onto the stage and was transfixed with fear. The piano played my introduction, and when I opened my mouth to sing, nothing came out. The princess leaned over to Prince Rainier and said, "I wonder why they chose this lad? He doesn't seem to be able to sing at all; he can't even speak!" The next morning I woke in a fright, and had to endure that anxiety throughout the day. Once at the concert hall, we were ushered to a room backstage to be personally introduced to the prince and princess before the performance. I had always regarded Princess Grace as the living image of a fairy-tale princess, and when she entered the room, she fulfilled everything that I had imagined. From the hem of her sweeping pink gown to her diamond tiara, she was an absolutely breathtaking sight. I was so overwrought in her presence that I could barely squeeze her gloved hand when it was my turn to greet her. Luckily I found my composure, and my dream of the night before did not become a reality. I sang well, and enjoyed myself immensely as one of the young performers entertaining our country's most eminent guests.

The Féis continued to be an exciting singing event throughout my student years. While a student at the Academy of Music, one of my most memorable competitions was the Silver Rose Bowl for Lieder Singing in the Féis Ceoil *(kee-ohl)* in Dublin. Father Lawless and I were great admirers of the German Lieder singers Dietrich Fisher-Dieskau, Hans Hotter, and Herman Prey, and we worked very hard to prepare for this particular Féis. I studied the German language diligently, taking great care in pronunciation and learning the meanings of all the words in the songs. When my round of singing was finished, I felt I had done fairly well. Although everyone advised against it, I had sung Schubert's "Serenade" for my recall number because I loved the song dearly. I have always believed that it's the feeling one has toward a piece that makes it effective for the audience—not how flashy the song is itself. This attitude served me well then, and I believe it accounts for the popularity of my performances and recordings to this day.

I took a seat beside Father Lawless to listen to the judge announce the third and second runners-up, and finally the winner. The two runners-up were very well-known singers in Dublin at the time, and far more experienced than I. But I was still disappointed to not have been among them, because I thought I had done well enough for third, at least. With the suspense over, I relaxed in my seat and awaited the announcement of the first-place winner. The judge read the winner's marks, and I was amazed that someone had earned such impressively high points. But the most astonishing fact was yet to come—the highest scoring winner was me! Thrilled and proud and happy, I brought my gleaming silver trophy home to my mother, who was ill in bed and could not attend the Féis.

Shortly after winning this prize, the German Institute of Cultural Relations in Dublin invited me to perform a full Lieder recital. My two-and-a-half-hour program consisted of songs by all the major Lieder composers, including Beethoven, Brahms, Schumann, Wolf, and of course, Schubert. The concert was such a success that I received glowing reviews in the Dublin newspapers and was offered a scholarship to study music full-time in Germany. I didn't take that scholarship, however, because my mother felt that I should prepare for a steady job in case the singing career could not support me. She didn't doubt my ability to become a professional singer, but she was concerned that the work may not be as secure as another profession.

A wealthy Belgian woman named Madam Ithier invited me to do another Lieder recital in Brussels. The trip to Belgium had a rough start—it was the first time I ever got airsick— but the program I sang for Flemish Radio went beautifully, and the elderly Madam Ithier treated me like a prince. Her lavish home and dinner table, laden with gold-and-silver cutlery and gold goblets, was quite a sight for a young lad from Terenure. I often wonder what might have developed from further contact with Belgian radio and television, backed by Madam Ether's strong admiration for my talent. Unfortunately, I was too young at the time to know anything about career development.

All I wanted to do was sing. Anywhere, anytime, for anyone!

Chapter Two

Music and Medicine

There was never any question that I would continue studying voice and performing, yet I took my mother's advice to heart, and began to study dentistry at the University of Dublin as my brother Thomas had done before me. I wasn't opposed to entering some field of medicine, but as I got into my studies I realized dentistry wasn't my cup of tea. In fact, I hated it. So I took the lead of another successful brother, Donal, and began an Optician's course at the College of Technology in Dublin. I soon found optics much more interesting than dentistry, and I felt confident I could make it through the four-year course.

All through my ophthalmology studies I continued to study singing, and was far more enthusiastic about it than my medical career. My musical colleagues and I earned our money singing all types of concerts: golf dinners, charity concerts, household recitals, and most of all, weddings and funerals. Weddings were a tremendous and reliable source of income, because in the busiest months I could sing one or two during the week and three or four ceremonies each day of the weekend. It was a hectic situation, literally running from one church to another but it was a welcome way to earn money. It is a rewarding thing now, twenty-five and thirty years later, to be approached after a concert by a couple whose wedding I sang for back in those days. I cannot remember them—not because it's been so many years—but because I never saw their faces! I only saw their backs as they marched down the aisle, and by the time they turned around to march back out I was already off to the next ceremony!

We also sang many concerts for the Red Cross, in hospitals and prisons. I will never forget the fresh face of one young man who sat in the front row at one of our concerts in a hospital for the criminally insane. His bright, smiling face was full of enthusiasm for every song our group of singers and musicians performed, and he applauded wildly for each piece. Afterward, I asked the doctor if this boy would be in for long; it seemed a shame that such a lovely boy should be incarcerated with such dangerous and unstable criminals. The doctor said he was sure the boy would be staying for quite a while, seeing that he had hacked his mother to death with an axe. I didn't ask questions about my audience at the Red Cross concerts after that.

There were lighthearted surprises at charity concerts, too. One evening a group of us sang at a home for unmarried mothers which was run by the nuns. One of the members of our troupe walked onstage and proceeded to break into song with "One Night of Love." There was utter pandemonium backstage as we tried to pull her offstage, and the sisters were absolutely furious. The poor singer hadn't given the words a thought.

Golf dinners paid well, yet were sometimes hairy occasions for singing. Often the guests would have played a game of golf and come into the club for a few whiskeys or Irish coffees, and it would be nine or ten o'clock in the evening before they'd settle down for dinner. They were happy indeed by this time, and loved to sing along with my songs. I took myself very seriously at that stage, far too seriously, and found it dreadful to have the entire room singing along to such long-practiced songs as "You Are My Heart's Delight." But I always got paid—anything from three guineas to five pounds—which was good money in the 1960s. So I put up with the jolly fellows.

One evening, halfway through a concert at the Border Inn in a town called Newry, on the border between Southern and Northern Ireland, the audience simply got up and started for the doors. "I can't be *that* bad," I thought to myself as I watched them file out. The manager called me off the stage, gave me my money, and told me to immediately get to my car and drive away, because they had had a bomb scare. My girlfriend Anne and I got in the car and drove as fast as we could. We had been on the road for no more than ten minutes when I saw a huge flash in the rearview mirror, which was the Border Inn being blown to bits. In the many years that I lived in Ireland, this was the only incidence of the country's problems that ever came close to my life.

In addition to the concerts and weddings, I was very active in musical comedy during my years in ophthalmology school. These shows included *Rosemarie*, *Magyar Melody*, *Carousel* and *South* Pacific. Upbeat, well-loved musicals were a lot of fun because they combined singing with acting. And acting is another word for hamming it up, which is why most of us wanted to be onstage in the first place. My absolute favorite roles among these musicals were Emile DeBeque in *South Pacific* and Billy Bigelow in *Carousel*.

The musical-comedy experience was important as well as fun because I could use the songs in my dinner concerts. The last thing a room full of men fresh off the golf course would want to hear would be German Lieder! So the show songs and standards such as "Jeannie of the Light Brown Hair" were my bread-and-butter songs while I put myself through ophthalmology school.

I made my operatic debut at the Wexford Festival of Opera, an internationally famous festival in Wexford, Ireland, held every year during the months of October and November. My first operatic performances were in Stanford's *Much Ado About Nothing* and Balfe's *The Siege of LaRochelle*. I didn't find these to be very interesting operas, and was much more excited to later sing in Verdi's *Il Trovatore* in Galway.

Radio Eireann, as Irish radio was called, provided me with some wonderful performing experiences at this time with their program entitled "Newcomers to the Microphone." Standing behind the live mike of a radio studio gave me the chance to feel like a real professional, as it did for many other young singers.

These were wonderful years of singing—in concerts, at dinners, for charity events, on little radio spots, and of course, competing in the festivals.

Eventually it was final examination time, and I had to gear up for a grueling series of orals and practical tests in ophthalmology. About ten days before the tests were to begin, my good friend Kevin Blake and I were standing on the eighth tee at the Killiney Golf Club. Kevin looked at me and said, "You know, John, we've only got ten days until the finals." So after the game we put our clubs away and began to study. Only something this important—barring a full-scale natural disaster—could keep us off the golf course for two precious weeks.

One of the exams took place the morning after the recital I had given at the German Institute of Cultural Relations. There was a review and large photograph of me in the *Irish Times*, which the test adjudicator was reading while we were writing our exams. For some people, art and medicine don't mix. I will never forget how he shook his head and gave me an incriminating look over his reading glasses, as if to say, "How dare this young man have the cheek to spend the night singing, when he should have been studying like crazy!"

But my singing persona came in quite handy during another part of the examinations. The Department of Ophthalmology of Ireland would employ ladies to come in and have their eyes tested by the students, as a diagnostic part of the finals. These ladies each had particular eye defects, and it was our challenge to diagnose them correctly. The woman I was examining was a lovely Dublin lady who recognized me from some concerts she had attended. She was hired to come in because she had a highly unusual prescription in each eye. I figured out the condition of the right eye, but I was completely stumped about the left. I began to spell out the prescription, and she very politely leaned over and said, "Mr. MacNally, that's the wrong prescription." She proceeded to correct me, and said she just wanted to look after me in case I made a mistake. I never dreamed that my singing could help me through my optics exams, but I certainly didn't mind!

In 1963, I was fortunate to pass all my examinations and qualify as an ophthalmic optician. I opened a practice, and my patient list grew quickly. Because it gave me a chance to meet, talk and work with people, optics gave me great enjoyment as a profession, and also filled me with a rewarding sense of helping people.

I had been in business two years when I decided to marry Anne, the love of my life since I first met her at a dance on June 27, 1959. When I went home and announced my intentions in the kitchen, everyone burst out laughing. The thought of the baby of the family getting married—a lad who didn't have two pennies to rattle on a tombstone—was too much. But once they picked themselves up from the floor and pulled themselves together, they realized how serious I was, and Anne and I were married on May 1, 1965.

A tremendous thing happened for my singing career in the year I got married. I got a phone call from Fred O'Donovan, the original producer of the famed Jury's Hotel cabaret in Dublin.

He was anxious to sign me on, and I signed a contract to sing seven shows per week for fifteen pounds per week. Anne and I had just bought a lovely new home in Terenure, and our payments were twenty pounds per month. With weekly wages of fifteen pounds, the equivalent of about thirty dollars, coming in from just one source, it felt like we had found our pot of gold!

Jury's was packed every night, seven nights a week, for six months out of the year. This great cabaret presented famous and accomplished Irish artists such as Alma Carroll and the Young Dublin Singers; Albert Le Bas, the magician; Cecil Nash, the singing chef; tenor Edmund Browne; and the wonderful ventriloquist Eugene Lambert. Eugene and his wife had ten children, and he always said they were all supported by his dummy, Finnegan. Jury's was the favorite with American tourists, but there were other successful cabarets in Dublin, too. Throughout the next two years, I also performed regularly at the Gaiety Theater and the new Dolphin Inn. Suddenly I was running an optician's business and singing in four venues at once: Jury's Hotel for the lunch show, and the Gaiety Theater, Dolphin Inn, and Jury's Hotel at night. These three establishments were all within walking distance of one another, and some days I found myself running from one to the other at such a pace that I expected to meet myself on the way back! But it was wonderful work, because I loved it and it eliminated any financial problems young married couples usually have.

During tourism's off-season, when the Dublin cabarets were closed, I went to England to work in the clubs. "Work" is an understatement; "sweat blood" may be more appropriate. Trying to break into show business in England was more than difficult; the fierce competition and tough audiences knocked the corners off a performer.

The audiences in the northern cities are particularly rough. One season I worked in a place called the Manchester City

Football Club, singing between the bingo games. After a game, the losers were so disgusted or depressed they didn't want to listen to me, and those who won were at the bar buying beers and carrying on so loudly they *couldn't* listen to me. One night, halfway through a song, the emcee leapt onto the stage, grabbed the microphone from my hand and yelled, "Now listen, you bloody lot, shut up and listen to the singer!" Unnerving experiences like these were common in the English clubs.

On another occasion I was sent to the 99 Club in Barrow-In-Furnace, a town where they were building submarines in secret. What a seedy dive! Once again, I might as well have stayed home, because I followed a stripper who did an act with a live snake, leaving nothing to the imagination. By the time I got onstage, the men were so worked up they had no interest in me, and came close to throwing beer bottles at the stage.

I sang in many clubs in the Manchester/Liverpool area to audiences who would eat you without salt if you weren't any good. And even if you were, they'd still hate you if they weren't in good humor that particular evening. There was one beautiful club in Manchester, however: The Talk of the North. This large, gorgeous place was an imitation of The Talk of the Town in London, where I had also sung. But The Talk of the North had problems getting an audience. When I started there were eight artists in the cabaret, including Jane Russell. Lack of customers made the roster drop to two by the end of the week, leaving just me and Jane. The biggest audience we had in a night numbered eight people, making it an incredibly bad experience for everyone concerned.

My work in the English clubs left me very disenchanted with cabaret. Although all my experiences in the Dublin cabarets were much more positive, I'll never love that form of entertainment.

While I was working in England in 1967 and 1968, I was very keen on landing a recording contract. A few years earlier I had recorded a series of musical-comedy albums in London, including *Naughty Marietta* and *Desert Song*. Even though we were just paid a straight fee and did not receive any royalties, it was great to be asked to make these records. But in 1967 and 1968 the situation was reversed: I was going to the record companies—they weren't coming to me. I visited fourteen record companies in London, and if there is one event that taught me that persistence is everything, it is the day I proceeded on to number fifteen. I walked in to CBS Records and asked if there was any possibility I could play a demonstration tape for Reg Wharburton. At the time, this gentleman was recording the ethnic music of England, Scotland, Ireland, and Wales on a new set of albums called the Inheritance Series. Reg listened to my tape, liked it, and asked me to come back that very afternoon. When I returned, he offered me a contract!

This experience and many since then have taught me the immeasurable value of persistence. I often turn to a quote that sums up a philosophy that has been proven again and again in my life:

> *Nothing in the world can take the place of persistence. Talent will not; nothing is more common than unsuccessful men with talent. Genius will not; unrewarded genius is almost a proverb. Education alone will not, the world is full of educated derelicts. Persistence and Determination alone are Omnipotent.*

Talent is just the beginning. As Ray Charles of the Ray Charles Singers once told me while he was writing some charts, "You know, John, you have a magnificent voice, that's your gimmick.

Now let's forget about that and work on these lyrics." Talent is the given element, and hard work and persistence are equally if not more important ingredients in becoming a good singer.

I suggested to CBS Records that we should also record a beautiful song I had been singing with We 4. This group was made up of three lads and one girl. The top lad was Larry Hogan, and the girl was Suzanne Murphy, who is now a famous opera star. The song, "Mary in the Morning," had previously been recorded by Al Martino, and I got raves when I performed it back home at the Dolphin Inn. CBS listened, and loved it. I recorded "Mary in the Morning," and watched it climb the charts and become an enormous hit. In Ireland and everywhere, it was all a dream come true: every time you turned on the radio they were playing my song.

The popularity of that one hit led to a number of Irish radio series, a guest spot on the "Life of Reilly" television show, and my own television series, "The John MacNally Show." It was almost unbelievable to suddenly be thrust into the limelight of show business, and be given the opportunity to meet some famous and wonderful people. Bing Crosby came to Ireland in 1967 and 1968 to do a television program called "A Little Bit of Ireland," which would be released worldwide. I was booked as a guest on that show by Fred O'Donovan, the producer who gave me my first job at Jury's Hotel. It was fantastic to meet Bing Crosby and talk to him extensively about many things, including golf, which we both loved.

With exciting opportunities opening up in radio and television, and countless offers for singing engagements streaming in, I sold my optician's business in 1969 and delved into my professional singing career full-time.

The boy soprano with a hole in his trousers had made it to the top of the charts!

Chapter Three

The MacNally Clan

Patrick MacNally was a captain in the Irish Army when he married my mother, Elizabeth Gillen. A native of Belfast, my father was not a rich man, but managed to provide very well for his large family. Although he was strict with us, the extra things he did, such as growing tomatoes in a greenhouse in the backyard to earn a little extra money, were proof of his loving dedication to his family.

My mother was from Longford, in the Irish Midlands. She was actually born in New York, where her parents met, but was brought to Ireland at the age of two. Her mother was from Donegal, in the north of Ireland, and her father was from Longford. My mother was very musical, and was blessed with a beautiful singing voice. It is easy to recall the house being filled with the sound of her lovely singing voice one of her favorite songs: "What will I do when you are far away/And I am blue/ What will I do?" Being the youngest child, I was her baby, and we were extremely close. She was an enormously sympathetic and kind person who always believed in me, gave me her full support, and instilled in me her strong faith.

My mother passed away in 1961 from cancer, and her death was a terrible blow to all of us. Because of how close we were, this was one of the darkest periods of my life. Her death was a great loss, and it took me a long time to recover from it.

Father survived her for seventeen years, until he died in 1978. My mother and my father were wonderful parents to all of us, and my memories of growing up on Fortfield Road are very happy ones.

When my brother Donal and I were boys we spent many summer holidays with our mother's sister, Aunt Mollie, and our grandmother at their home in Longford. I always remember Grandmother as very old, and very funny. She never wore glasses, and she could still read her prayer book in her eighties. Two wild, scatterbrained boys living under her roof for five to six weeks must have worn her to a frazzle. I know she was relieved to see us leave, because when we were finally put on the bus to return home, we would stick our heads out the window to say good-bye and hear her say, "Good-bye now, and God be with you on the Dublin Road. *And don't come back!*"

We have great memories of those holidays, as well as the ones we spent with my father's sister and her husband, Aunt Sadie and Uncle Jack, in Belfast.

My eldest brother is Terence, who eagerly awaited the end of his school days so that he could wander around England before settling down. Once he did settle down, he returned to school to study podiatry (chiropody, as it is known in Ireland), and has developed one of the most successful practices in the country. He and his wife Rita have two beautiful children and make their home in Dublin.

The second-eldest child is Patrick. After moving to the United States at a young age, he joined the American Army and fought in the Korean War. I was convinced that it was Pat I saw up on

My mother and I
at our home in Dublin.

The Mac Nally Clan.
L to R: Patrick, Terence with me on his knee, Thomas, Sheila, Donal (under the high stool).

This picture was taken after I had won the Feis Ceoil in Dublin. I was 9 years old.

Posing proudly with my first girlfriend Claire Dowling (left) and her sister Terri, who lived two doors down from us in Fortfield Road.

Taken in 1987 at The National Concert Hall in Dublin. One of the rare occasions when the whole family was together in one place, in front of William Orpin's painting of Count John Mc Cormack. L to R: Donal, Terence, Sheila, Thomas, meself, Patrick (with eyes closed specially for the picture!!!).

My parents Patrick and Elizabeth on their wedding day in St. Michael's Catholic Church, Dunlaoghaire, Co. Dublin, 1927.

With my parents in Dublin 1956.

The day of my qualification as an Ophthalmic Optician. I am seated first on the left in the front row, my good friend and golfing partner Kevin Blake is fourth from the left in the back row.

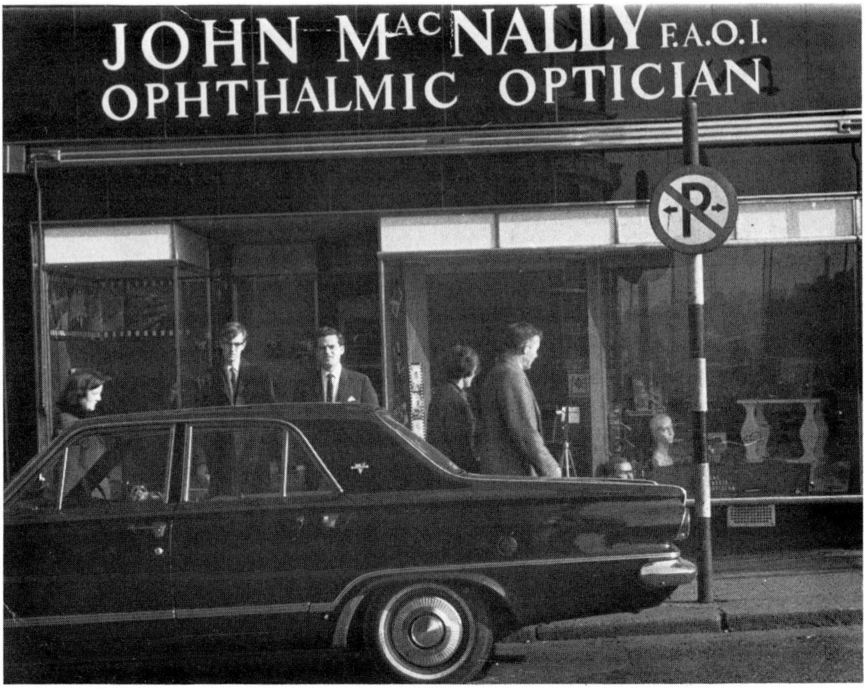

JOHN MacNALLY F.A.O.I.
OPHTHALMIC OPTICIAN

The opening of my optical practice at 2 Capel St., Dublin in 1967 where I practiced until I turned fulltime professional singer in 1969. That is my car parked under the no parking sign!

An early promotion photo.

1st of May, 1965, the happiest day of my life. Anne and I in the wedding car immediately after our wedding mass in St. Joseph's Church in Terenure, Dublin.

Colonel Austin X. Lawlor and Mrs. Margaret Lawlor, Anne's parents, pictured in Dublin circa 1973.

As Count Di Luna in Verdis Opera Il Trovatore, performed in Tuam Co. Galway during our honeymoon. I had previously made my operatic debut at the Wexford Festival of Opera, an internationally famous festival that continues today.

With Elizabeth and Austin in our home in Dublin, circa 1972.

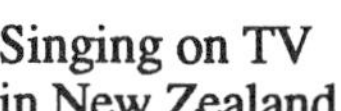

Singing on TV in New Zealand.

Farewell appearance in Westfield Shopping Centre in Sydney before departing for Las Vegas.

Singing the Australian Trilogy to 90,000 people before a football match in Perth, Australia.

On the beach in Newport, Sydney, with Jack Neary, at one time the most influential entrepreneur in Australia and a great help to my career in that country, also a close friend. He was responsible for bringing the Beatles to Australia.

With Cyril Count Mc Cormack (son of the great Irish tenor Count John Mc Cormack) in Dublin, circa 1966.

With Cyril again after a concert in Dublin in 1994, he is presenting me with a gold jewelry box owned by his father for my services to the John Mc Cormack Society.

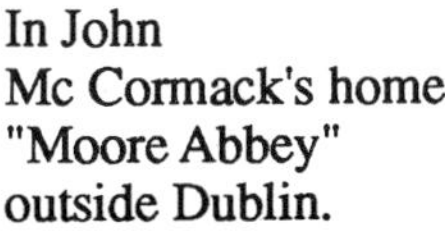

In John Mc Cormack's home "Moore Abbey" outside Dublin.

Arriving in Dublin in Dec. '94 for my first concert there in 12 years, being welcomed by L to R: Mrs. Lawlor (wife of the Australian Ambassador to Ireland and the Vatican), Michael O'Halloran (Lord Mayor of Dublin), Sir Peter Lawlor (the Ambassador), my brother Donal.

Backstage at the National Concert Hall Dublin, Dec. '94.
L to R: Austin, Anne, me, Elizabeth.

On stage, National Concert Hall, Dublin.

Arus An Uachtarain (home of the president of Ireland). L to R: Elizabeth, Patrick Hillery (President of Ireland), and "meself". "Afternoon Tea".

After presidential command performance in Sydney, Australia.
L to R: Mary Lee, Cardinal Sir James Freeman, Doctor Hillery, me, Alderman Douglas Sutherland (Lord Mayor of Sydney). I presented this Australian painting to the president after the concert. 1985.

Taken in Sydney with my accompanist Moira Briody who died suddenly a few years later.

With Anne, Fred and Sally O'Donnovan. Fred has for many years produced my concerts in Dublin and came to Sydney to produce the presidential concert at the Town Hall. This was the first ever visit by an Irish president while in office, to Australia.

After the official signing of the scholarship we gave to the Conservatorium of Music in Sydney, from monies received at the Presidential Concert. L to R: Terry Molloy (one of my long time friends in Sydney), Cardinal Sir James Freeman, "meself", Jack Chown (my great old "Aussie Mate"), Rev. Father Don Willoughby, our good friend and parish priest of St. Patrick's Church in Bondi, Sydney.

Making Irish coffee in Sydney, 1972. Key word: "Concentration"!!!

My greatest sporting passion (always wanted to be a golf professional—secret ambition!)

Two of Australia's greatest golfing legends, with whom I played many a round. Norman Von Nida and Kel Nagle.

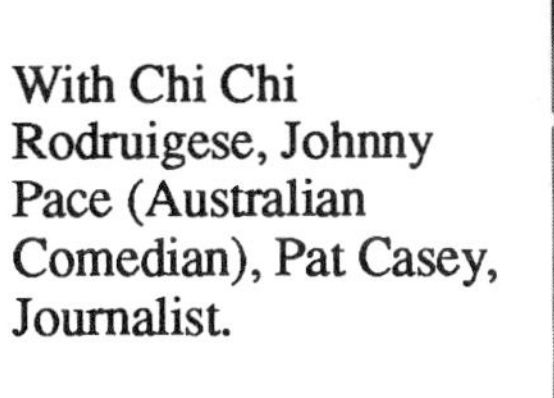

With Chi Chi Rodruigese, Johnny Pace (Australian Comedian), Pat Casey, Journalist.

Nothing like a round of golf. Taken at Nashville Golf and Athletic Club.

After a golf tournament in Ireland. L to R: Joe Carr, legendary Irish golf amateur; my brother Donal, Ireland's greatest and best known golfer with whom I have had the honour of playing many a round both in Ireland and Australia; Christy O'Connor, and "meself".

With Henry Mancini in Dublin after I had recorded one of his many wonderful songs, this one was from a film and was titled "Loss of Love".

Engaged at the Sahara Hotel, Las Vegas. I became the first Irish born singer to sing solo in a showroom in Vegas.

Taken backstage at the Sahara. L to R: Buddy Hackett (on who's show I appeared), Jim Nabors, me, Sahara executive.

SUNDAY WORLD, July 15, 1973

SHOW - BIZ WORLD

John McNally pictured with Liberace

I met Liberace during the 1974 Jerry Lewis Telethon. He was a kind and supportive man who made a special effort to spread his high opinion of my singing among his many friends and contacts.

I became close friends with Jack Benny during one of his visits to Las Vegas. He was marvellous company, very polite and charming and one of the nicest men I have ever met in showbusiness.

Telly Savalas and I met in Los Angeles. He would soon see brighter and better and busier days with the launch of his hit series "Kojak".

During my Elvis era in Las Vegas. "All very hard to do... lots of effort."

With Johnny Mathis after a game of golf at the Australian Golf Club in Sydney. That's my two dollars. I won the game.

In Australia I was fortunate to share a concert with the great American operatic tenor Jan Peerce.

Backstage with Jan Peerce. We had many long chats about singing. He was a leading tenor with the New York Metropolitan Opera for forty years.

Singers together, Operatic Baritone Robert Allman is one of the leading baritones with the Australian Opera Company, a golf nut, and a very good friend.

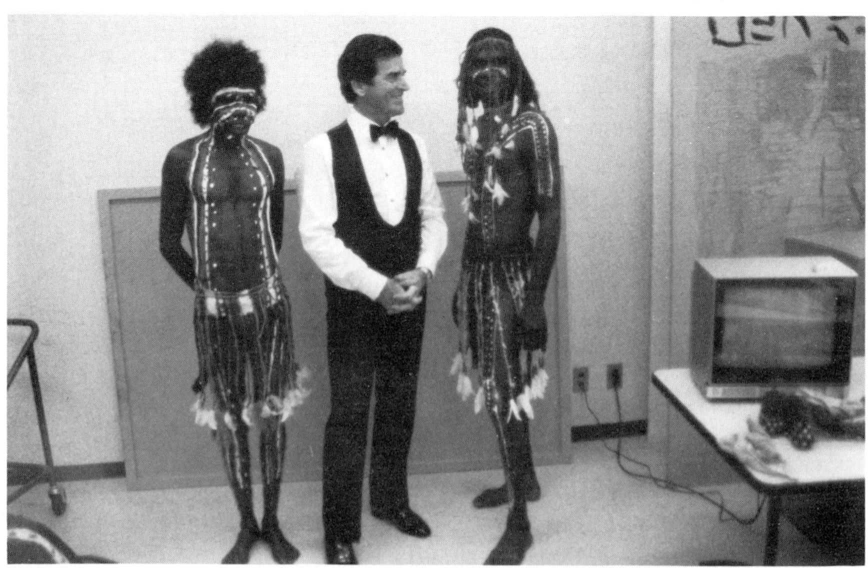

Representing Australia at World's Fair in Japan 1984, pictured with two Aboriginal dancers from the Northern Territory, in Australia. The one on my left is David Gullipill who starred with Paul Hogan in "Crocodile Dundee". He is a brilliant dancer.

With the mayor of New York, Ed Koch, after a radio show on St. Patrick's Day in New York.

Backstage at the Grand Ole Opry in Nashville, with the lovely lady and country comedienne Minnie Pearl.

On stage with Minnie Pearl and Roy Acuff. I had just been introduced to the audience by Minnie after she had heard me on the TNN Show "Nashville Now".

In Roy Acuff's dressing room after the show.

At the interview desk with Ralph Emery in July '93. I have been a regular on that show since 1987. Now it has changed to "Music City Tonight" with Crook and Chase with whom I have appeared many times.

Taken in July '92.

With
Cristy Lane
in Branson,
Missouri.

With Glen
Campbell in
Branson, during a
golf tournament.

With Andy Williams in Branson, Missouri in '93. Andy's show is one of the best shows you will see anywhere—very professional.

Taken at "FanFair" with Norm Anderson.

During the filming of my Irish special on the "General Jackson Riverboat" in Nashville. L to R: Norm Anderson, Anne, Bill Walker.

In the recording studios at Nashville.

In my dressing room at Westbury Music Fair in Long Island, with one of my best friends John Braunschweig and his wife Carole.

After singing at an ecumenical service in St. Varton's Cathedral, New York. L to R: Me, Archbishop Mannogian, Head of the Armenian Church in the U.S., Cardinal Willebrands.

With my lovely Elizabeth.

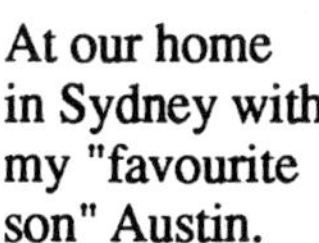

At our home in Sydney with my "favourite son" Austin.

Still in the backyard of our home in Sydney, taken by Anne. L to R: Austin, David and Cheryle Owen (Our good friends who live in our street) and "meself".

Elizabeth's 21st. birthday party in Sydney. Theme of the party, "Dressed to Kill".

Taken at the "Alamo" in San Antonio, Texas, before a concert there in '92. I was amazed and delighted to see the names of so many Irish men and women who fought and died at the "Alamo".

"What are you doing here" with sculpture of Irish poet Patrick Kavanagh beside the canal in Dublin, the subject of so many of his poems.

"Just a nice shot" taken by one of the members of the fan club at Valley Forge Music Fair in Philadelphia.

Usual panic after a concert. NCH Dublin.

"Just a minute, John".

the silver screen one day when my pals and I were at the cinema. The Pathe Movietone News segment about the war showed a soldier helping a wounded man onto a stretcher, and I immediately recognized the soldier as my brother Pat. I got the entire family to come and see it, and there was quite a discussion about whether it was him or not. I still believe it was. Pat now lives in Ireland, and he and his wife Jeanette have two children.

Sheila is the only girl in the family, and with a strong will of her own she had no difficulty holding her ground among five boys. After finishing school, and much to my parents' amazement and delight, Sheila announced her plans to join the Cross and Passion Order, and became a nun. She studied nursing in London, and after completing her degree went to Africa, where she served for close to twenty years. From Africa she went to Chile, where she still lives and serves with the order. Sheila comes home to Ireland every three or four years, and during my mother's illness it was a great comfort to the entire family when she returned to take care of her. She has been in Chile for many years, and we are all immensely proud of the wonderful work she is doing.

The third MacNally son is Thomas, who was an excellent student, and a great flirt with the girls. Thomas studied dentistry at University College in Dublin, and upon his qualification opened a practice close to our home in Terenure. Later he obtained a post as a dentist in the Irish Army, moved up the ranks to Lieutenant Colonel, and he is now head of the Irish Army Dental Corps. His position has taken him on assignments to the Middle East for the United Nations. Thomas is also an accomplished violinist, and plays in several string ensembles, some of which have toured in the United States. After a concert, I value Thomas' criticism and feedback, knowing that it comes from an excellent musician. He and his wife Ruth have six children and live in the very house we grew up in on Fortfield Road.

Donal is the brother closest to me in age. As a boy soprano, I was always in Donal's shadow, as he was a magnificent, beautiful singer, and one of the finest Ireland has ever produced. The American press hailed him as the best boy soprano in the world of his time. Donal participated in all the festivals, and was a very prominent and sought-after young singer. But his gift mysteriously left him when his voice broke, and never came back. It has always amazed us that our voices broke within a couple of years of each other, but the result has been so different for each of us.

Donal began his professional life working in the hotel business in Dublin, and he impressed everyone as a dapper young man with a charismatic personality. He began to study ophthalmology in night school, and shortly after qualifying and opening his own practice, he set up shop on Mary Street in the center of Dublin. Everyone advised against buying this particular practice because it was so run-down, but Donal went on to make it one of the most flourishing practices in Dublin. He is now the premier ophthalmic optician in Ireland, with many practices and a great deal of respect in the business. He and his wife Carolyn have six children and live in Dublin.

Donal is my closest brother and best friend. We have been through a lot together, and we love to talk about music. Donal is an exceptionally gifted musician, an absolute natural who plays violin and piano with equal dexterity. He has accompanied me on many occasions, and does an incredible job arranging my concerts in Ireland.

Musical evenings at home were a common event with my family in Ireland. For family and friends who didn't have a chance to sing in public, it was a time to sing the songs they just loved to sing. Sometimes I'd bring a special guest, like the baritone who was singing in *Rigoletto* one year, Piero Cappuccilli, whose beautiful voice captivated me completely. Having him sing in my home was absolutely wonderful. An interesting fact about that particular *Rigoletto* production is that the tenor was Luciano Pavarotti—the not-yet-superstar, struggling artist Pavarotti. He was discovered in this Irish production by an agent who got him to replace the ailing Giuseppe di Stefano at Covent Garden soon afterward, and the opportunity made him very, very famous. But you didn't have to be a great artist to sing in our family musical evenings, it was just a bit of fun. Sometimes we would have the evenings at the home of one of my great friends, Des White, whose dog would have to be let out because he howled as soon as someone started singing, and on some evenings we held them in the home of another good friend, Jimmy O'Reilly. Unfortunately, the habit has all but died out. The fun is only revived when I return to Ireland and get together with family and friends in Dublin.

My wife, Anne Lawlor, grew up on Greenlea Road in the same part of Dublin as the MacNally family. I've been in love with Anne since we first met at the Templeogue Tennis Club dance, and she is my best friend and greatest support. She is a pillar of strength, and has done a miraculous job keeping our family together—a difficult task with a husband whose work takes him away from home for weeks and months at a time. In the years that we lived in Ireland, I grew very close to her wonderful parents, Colonel Austin X. Lawlor and Margaret Lawlor, and spent many happy hours at their home on Greenlea Road. It was the Lawlors who advised us to buy a house rather than rent a flat when we were first married, and we were happy we did. They've given us a lot of good advice, and plenty of love.

The house on Templeville Road was a very important home for us, and there were many wonderful happenings there. One particular incident my family and my neighbors will never let me forget happened early one cold winter morning. I got out of bed and ran across the cold floor to make a visit to the bathroom. When I was ready to go back to bed, I turned the key to get out, and the key would not turn. For love nor money, I could not t-urn that key. I forced it, I did everything to it, but it was stuck in the lock and wouldn't budge. Shivering in my underwear, I was trapped in that unheated bathroom for at least two hours. Everybody tried to get me out, but with no luck. Anne would slide a cigarette and a match underneath the door (I was still smoking at the time), and the glow of the cigarette was the only thing I had to keep me warm, which wasn't very much. So there I was, star of stage, screen, and radio in Ireland, stuck in the toilet in me underjacks, freezing with cold. Anne's mother came over to see if there was anything she could do, and although they deny it vehemently, I swear to this day that when I was alone in that bathroom, in the dead of winter, teeth chattering with the cold, I heard muffled giggling outside that door. Eventually we had to call the fire brigade. And, of course, the fire brigade arrived with bells and lights and sirens, and three husky fellows came up the stairs in full battle dress. They put a crowbar in the door and opened it, to reveal me standing there, freezing, almost naked. It took them a lot of willpower to keep the smiles off their faces. I walked out, put on my dressing gown, and took them down and gave them some Irish coffee, and had a hot cup of coffee myself to warm up, and made them swear that they would not reveal what had happened at the MacNally household that morning.

Every one of the neighbors asked Anne if anything serious had happened with the fire brigade, and after she told them the whole story they would come to me, pretending not to know anything, and without a smile on their faces ask me the same question—"Ah, John I saw the fire brigade coming to your house. Is everything all right?"—knowing damn well what had happened.

That's one episode on Templeville Road that created a lot of talk afterward, and a lot of laughter, and a lot of good stories. And as the ,years go on, the stories naturally become embellished.

Our house became a real home with the birth of our first child, Elizabeth, on January 26, 1966. Our son Austin was born on August 13 of the following year. It was heartbreaking to be away from Anne and my two beautiful children when my career took me far from home. The many rewards of singing to audiences throughout the world could not make up for the time I missed with Elizabeth and Austin when they were very young. But Anne had the love and strength to do the job of both parents, and it is because of her that we maintained a close and happy family home.

Since the children have grown up and moved on, Anne has been free to join me in all my travels, and it is a wonderful way of life for both of us. As I always say when I introduce the song, Anne is truly "The Wind Beneath My Wings."

Chapter Four

Taking Off "Down Under"

The success of "Mary in the Morning" was a turning point in my life, and I am still amazed to think of the effect one hit song can have on a career.

Just as amazing, and something to which I have given much thought throughout my career, is the art of singing, and the voice itself. Whenever I hear a singer, no matter what part of the world he or she may be in, I marvel at this wondrous, fantastic instrument. When I wake up in the morning and can sing again, I'm as excited as if it were the first time. When I was young, especially after my brother Donal's voice broke, I often wondered why one person would have a good voice and another couldn't sing at all. I've now come to realize that the voice is a gift from God. Without that gift, you've not got a singer's voice. When you get a gift it's always a nice thing to say thank you, and very few days go by in my life that I don't thank God for my voice. It's my whole life, and I've completely dedicated myself to it.

The words to one of my favorite songs, the well-loved hymn "How Great Thou Art," describes my feelings about this gift, and the faith that has kept me going in good times and bad:

O Lord my God! When I in awesome wonder
Consider all the works Thy hands have made,
I see the stars, I hear the rolling thunder,
Thy pow'r throughout the universe displayed,
Then sings my soul, my Savior God to Thee;
How great Thou art!

When through the woods and forest glades I wander
And hear the birds sing sweetly in the trees;
When I look down from lofty mountain grandeur
And hear the brook and feel the gentle breeze:
Then sings my soul, my Savior God to Thee;
How great Thou art!

When Christ shall come with shout of acclamation
And take me home, what joy shall fill my heart!
Then I shall bow in humble adoration
And there proclaim, my God, how great Thou art!
Then sings my soul, my Savior God to Thee;
How great Thou art!

Singing has given me great rewards, but it's truly a rollercoaster business: one moment you're up and the next moment You're down. You think you have an engagement and you don't, you think you have a record contract and you don't, or any number of dizzying expectations can knock you down into disappointment. It's at times like these that my faith is very important. When times are hard, and the whole world seems to be bearing down on me, I can turn to Him and get consolation from Him.

It takes something serious to prevent one from taking the gift of singing for granted, and one of a singer's greatest fears is that it may disappear. This, thank goodness, has happened me only once. Early in my career I sang the lead part of Edward Grieg in *The Song of Norway* in a production just outside Dublin. Being an immature singer at the time, I gave my full voice and full effort in each rehearsal, which is a great mistake. Only someone very green would be more concerned with being heard full-out every day than with saving the voice for the performance. On the opening Saturday night, which was also the night our daughter Elizabeth was born prematurely, I opened my mouth, and nothing happened. That was an absolutely staggering moment in my career. After something this traumatic happens and everything is right again, you realize just how lucky you are to have the gift of a voice.

"Mary in the Morning," the song that opened so many doors for me, eventually took me to the other side of the world.

One night in 1969, the head of the Irish Tourist Board in North America, Joe Malone, came to Jury's cabaret in Dublin. "Mary in the Morning" was already a hit in America, and after seeing and hearing me for himself, Mr. Malone invited me to join a group of artists to represent Ireland at the American Society of Travel Agents convention in Tokyo, Japan. Our cabaret at the Tokyo Hilton was an unqualified success, and for some reason the most popular of all the international shows at the convention. Perhaps it was the free Irish coffee!!

Whatever the reason, word spread throughout town that ours was the show to see, and a few of us were asked to sing in a concert for Emperor Hirohito. I was honored to sing for the occasion, and learned something about Japanese royal protocol that was a bit disconcerting at first. When I finished singing my first song, the hall was absolutely silent. After a long, uncomfortable pause, I began to walk off the stage, and suddenly the audience broke into applause. For a moment I thought they were applauding the fact that I was leaving, but I took a bow and received a very warm, enthusiastic response. I was told later that everyone must wait for the emperor to applaud first. He may take his time, but the audience has to take its cue from him.

At the close of the convention, I asked Joe Malone if he would mind if I made a trip to Australia on my way back to Ireland. I was dying to visit Australia, and I figured as long as I was this close—why not? The cabaret had been such a success that the Irish Tourist Board was happy to pay any extra travel expenses. I spent four weeks in Australia, escorted by Jack Neary, one of the top promoters in the entertainment business and a man who was to become one of my dearest friends.

Jack Neary was famous for bringing some of the biggest acts in show business to Australia. For example, when the Beatles had five records on the top-ten charts worldwide, Jack signed them to do an Australian tour. During my first visit, he went right to work and booked appearances on television programs and in several shows, including performances in the Celebrity Room in Melbourne.

I will never forget my first performance at the Celebrity Room in Melbourne. The afternoon before the performance, I was doing an interview with a journalist for one of the newspapers. I had to cut the interview short, because I suddenly had a terrible pain in my stomach. I went to my room at the hotel, and the dreadful pain grew worse and worse. I called the house doctor, who examined me and told me I had a kidney stone. He had to give me two injections of pathadene, a derivative of morphine, before the pain subsided. Luckily I passed the stone before the show that night, but the good doctor attended the performance with a loaded syringe in his bag, just in case.

In spite of the kidney stone, my first experience in Australia was fantastic, and I sensed it to be a place of great opportunity. I was very grateful to Jack for all he had done for me in such a short time, and as I left I told him I planned to return.

Filled with enthusiasm about Australia, I went home to Dublin and had a wonderful reunion with Anne and the family. My concert schedule in Ireland was still in full swing, and for the next two years I even produced some of my own shows. One particularly successful engagement was a series of concerts in the Cork Opera House, which drew such great audiences night after night that it broke all house attendance records.

It was at this time that I had an unfortunate experience with management. Sometimes I just insist on learning things the hard way. Due to poor judgment on my part, I had signed on with a man who did not have any experience in show business, but claimed to have a lot of contacts and influence. He tried to prevent my return to Australia, and caused me a lot of grief. Even though I won the court case that I had to bring against him, it took a lot of money and turned out to be a costly way of learning valuable lessons about contracts and management.

In 1971 I returned to Australia for a one-week tour. This time Jack Neary got me a spot on the "Tonight Show," a popular Saturday-night program hosted by Simon Dee. It had previously been hosted by Sebastian Cabot and a number of famous celebrities. I sang two songs on the program, and was interviewed by Mr. Dee about my career and the political situation in Ireland, which was something I did not care to discuss. But I managed to work around the questions, and the entire interview came out quite well.

For some reason, Simon Dee had a falling out with Channel 9 on the following Monday, and that week the station called and asked if I had any experience hosting a program such as the "Tonight Show." I told them that I had a lot of television experience, but had never interviewed anyone on the air. The Tonight Show" aired from 9:30 to 11:00 P.M., and although artists performed on the show, the host had a heavy responsibility for filling that time with interview questions and conversation. The station managers decided to take a chance, and asked me to fill in on the following Saturday night.

When I got off the phone I nearly died of nerves. It's one thing to be a guest on a show—sing your bit, chat a while, try to be charming and say, good-bye—but it's quite another thing to run the whole show. Nevertheless, in four days I would be on live television, interviewing guests I had never met in my life. I did my research, selected the most popular songs in my repertoire, and did the show. They must have thought it was a success, because they asked me to do it again the following week. So began my three-year job as host of the "Tonight Show," and I am proud of the fact that during my tenure in the host's chair the ratings were higher than ever before. Geoff Harvey, producer and musical director, and John Lane, director, were fantastic to work with, and we all became great friends. What a great way to jump into show biz, Australian style.

When the "Tonight Show" offered me a contract, I called Anne and told her to pack up the kids and come to Australia. How many women would take it completely in stride when her husband phones one morning and asks her to move across the world, with two small children? I often wonder what I did to deserve Anne, and I can't imagine what I would ever do without her. We bought a condominium beside the famous Bondi Beach in Sydney, and later bought a piece of land in Coogee, just two minutes from Coogee Beach, and built a house there. Not only did we enjoy our beautiful house, but we were surrounded by lovely neighbors. David and Cheryl Owen became good friends, and continue to very generously look after our business affairs whenever we are away from the country for any length of time.

In addition to the weekly "Tonight Show" appearances, my first three years in Australia were filled with work in clubs, theaters, the Sydney Opera House, and on radio and television over at ABC, the Australian Broadcasting Corporation. I performed throughout the country, from Perth to Melbourne, down to Tasmania, and even out to the country of New Zealand, and the Australian people took me into their hearts.

Traveling through this amazingly vast country, playing concerts set up by my manager, John Doyle, in dozens of remote, one-horse towns, I never knew what to expect. Some of the civic centers were new and comfortable, but many were old and in terrible shape. When my accompanist Nancy Hoskings and I arrived at a theater, our first priority was to check out the condition of the piano. At a place called Swan Hill on the new South Wales-Victoria border, the theater looked condemned as well as ancient. Small animals scurried into the corners as we walked onto the stage to get a closer look at the old upright piano. Not only was the paint peeling on the outside, the inside was littered with beer bottles and packets of cigarettes.

Nancy nearly fainted when she noticed that there were eight keys physically missing from the keyboard of the piano. Tied to the off-side leg of this monstrosity was a huge rope that connected it to a steel ladder backstage, and kept it far to one side of the stage. The theater manager explained that there had once been a concert in which the pianist played so forcefully that the piano slid off the stage and nearly killed two people in the front row! Since then, a council ordinance decreed that a rope be permanently attached to one leg of the piano. Thankfully, Nancy and I discovered another piano in a tea room off the main theater, and as it was in considerably better shape, got by with it.

At the theater in Albury, another small town on the New South Wales–Victoria border, I asked the stage manager to kindly polish the grand piano, which was covered with dust. When my pianist and I walked out to begin our concert, the piano had been polished all right, but the tin of polish and rag were left lying on top of it for all the world to see. I challenge any performer to gracefully begin a concert after first removing a greasy rag from atop the piano! Also, during that very concert, a workman in overalls ambled onto the stage, collected a stepladder from just behind the curtain at stage right, and casually left through the emergency-exit door without looking at anyone or saying a word. As I looked at him and looked back at the audience in disbelief, the entire place burst into gales of laughter.

Three very old Australian songs, "Waltzing Matilda," "The Road to Gundagai," and "Advance Australia Fair," which has since been adapted as the Australian national anthem, made up my Australian Trilogy. These songs were held in high esteem by the Australians, and I once had the opportunity to sing my Australian Trilogy in Perth in center field of a football arena filled with sixty thousand people.

No matter how large the crowd, the gift of singing that I mentioned earlier also carries a certain amount of responsibility. I have learned this through many moving experiences that have opened my heart to the effect my singing can have on another person's life. For example, when I was doing the "Tonight Show" in Australia, there was a girl who lived from week to week to see the show and to hear me sing the songs she loved. She couldn't move any muscle of her body, and she watched the show through a periscope. She was nineteen years old and had lived in the hospital her entire life.

There was another woman in Australia, Mary Burse, who was very ill and dying in the hospital. I knew Mary only as a nodding acquaintance in the crowd of fans who regularly greeted me after concerts. But with her family all around her bedside, she told them that her wish was to see me before she died. So the family phoned me, told me the situation, and I went to see her. She had lost a lot of weight, and was a very small figure in the bed. When I said, "Hello Mary, how are you?" she looked at me and rose up as if someone had taken her by the shoulders and pulled her. Although the doctor had given her about three days to live, six months later she was sitting in the front row of a concert I sang at the Sydney Opera House.

I once received a beautiful letter from a man named Lawrence Donohue in St. Paul, Minnesota, telling me how important my recordings had been to his family when their mother was dying in the hospital. She seemed to be comforted by the songs, and she passed away during the playing of "Danny Boy." Mr. Donohue wrote that the family played the tapes throughout the rest of that day and evening, and the music helped them get through a very sad day.

Incidents like these bring home the fact that singing is like a vocation, a calling. Even when things are tough and the entire music business seems crazy, I've felt a strong sense of commitment to what I'm doing with my life.

Although ninety-nine percent of my contacts in Australia have been extremely positive ones, every once in a while a person runs into someone who may be ready to take advantage of one's good faith. One of my least favorite experiences in Australia was the result of a rather poor business decision. One day a friend of mine approached me with his plan for a new pancake restaurant in Sydney. I became very caught up in his enthusiasm and believed that the operation would be successful, so I put up a considerable amount of money to become a partner. As the project unfolded, it became clear that the man didn't know anything about the restaurant business, and the entire enterprise ended up a complete failure.

Not only that, my "friend" packed up and disappeared overnight, owing many people an explanation—and a lot of money.

The moral of the story is to invest only in the business you know best, or in your own ability. Although I'll never consider myself a financial genius, I've learned many things through the years, and this hard-won lesson in good business sense was a dismal experience I will never repeat.

In spite of my one-time business failure, my family loved living in the land "down under," with its friendly, generous, and warmhearted people. This fascinating country and our many dear friends who live there will always be close to our hearts.

Chapter Five

On the Road in the U.S.A.

In 1973 the Irish Tourist Board contacted me in Sydney and asked me to represent Ireland at a convention in Las Vegas, a city I had heard much about, but had never visited. I knew it lit up a small part of the desert, and that it was unlike anywhere else in America—probably in the world. I also knew that for many people it was a mecca to see their legend and their king, Elvis Presley. Anxious to break into show business in the United States, I decided to take full advantage of my time in Las Vegas. My manager at the time, Mick Quinn of Dublin, hired a band and invited as many booking agents as he could find to come and listen to me.

The bookers came, and some were very interested, including Arvid Nelson of the Sahara Hotel. He needed an opening act for Buddy Hackett, and once Buddy Hackett heard me and approved of me, I got the job. With this engagement, I was the first Irish singer to perform solo in a showroom in Las Vegas.

Although Buddy Hackett came to hear me sing upon the invitation of Arvid Nelson, I didn't meet him at that time. My first introduction to Buddy was onstage during my first show at the Sahara. I had just sung my first song and was about to introduce my second when a small, fat man in a robe walked onstage and said, "Can you keep your voice down? I'm trying to take a nap in my dressing room!" The man was Buddy Hackett, of course, and the audience just broke up. His spontaneous entrance took me completely off guard. He asked if I was nervous, and I said, "No, not too nervous." Then he said, "Well, then why are you peeing on my foot?" This brought the house down once again, but it took me quite a while to regain my composure and smoothly continue my act. I was later told that he often makes such appearances during the opening act.

My success at the Sahara led to twenty-five continuous weeks in Las Vegas, performing additional shows at the Hilton with Myron Cohen and the Four Tops, and at the Flamingo Hotel. I also worked with the Association and the Mills Brothers, and my experiences with all these artists were very happy ones.

Just before I opened at the Las Vegas Hilton, the general manager suggested I go down to the showroom and watch Elvis Presley, who was headlining at the hotel. I wasn't keen on the idea, because I had never considered him a great singer. But I obliged the manager and attended his show that night. I was absolutely captivated. At such close range, I discovered Elvis had an extraordinary voice beneath the surface of the one he allowed to shine through. His act was incredible, and I enjoyed it so much I returned to see it sixteen times. Elvis sent me a Christmas card that year, and even though I believe he sent them to all the artists working at the Hilton, I was very proud of it.

While I was singing at the Hilton I came down with a cold, and made a visit to the Sunshine Medical Center that I will never forget. The doctor, who was also Elvis Presley's physician, treated me and told me to wait outside for a cab so I could get back to the hotel and get plenty of rest. As I stood by the curb, I watched idly as a car pulled into the clinic parking lot. The man in the passenger seat took something out of the glove compartment, put it into his mouth, and blew off the top of his head. I just stood there, stunned. The young driver of the car went berserk and was running all over the lot. As the other men from the car were pulling the body out, the doctor ran over to me and told me to leave, to quickly walk to the Hilton, because people would be showing up soon who would ask me a lot of questions if I hung around. Completely shaken, I walked back to the hotel. I searched through the Las Vegas newspapers for days after that incident, but never found a report of the death.

By far the most rewarding acquaintance I made in Las Vegas, and probably the most wonderful friendship I ever made in show business, was with Jack Benny. After the Sahara engagement, the organizers of the Jerry Lewis Telethon asked me if I would look after Mr. Benny for three days before his appearance on the program. Being one of his greatest admirers, I was absolutely thrilled at the thought of meeting and spending time with him. I picked him up at the airport, and during the next three days we spent hour after hour talking about music, our careers, and life in general, and we became very close friends. He told me about his ambitions to be a violinist, his friendship with the great violinist Isaac Stern, and the exciting concerts in which he had replaced Mr. Stern. I enjoyed Jack's company immensely. One morning he called my hotel room at two o'clock and asked, "What are you doing, John.'"

"Well, I'm in bed, Jack."

"In other words, you're not doing anything," he said. "Neither am I, so come on over and we'll have a nice conversation.

So I got dressed and went to his room and chatted for a couple of hours.

During one of our late-night talks, Jack told me a funny story about his famous reputation for being very cheap. One time when he arrived at the Las Vegas airport, he hopped into a cab and the cabbie recognized him. When they got to the hotel, the fare was about $2.50, and Jack gave the cabbie a ten-dollar bill and said, "You keep the change."

The driver looked at him, obviously confused, and said, "Aren't you Jack Benny'"

"Yes, I am," Jack said.

The cabbie counted out the change and gave it to Jack, saying, "I don't want you giving me that tip, because I want to tell my wife you were in my cab, and she'd never believe it was Jack Benny if I told her you gave me such a big tip!"

One night when I went to hear Jim Nabors' show in the Congo Room at the Sahara, a dreadful sound came from somewhere in the orchestra at the start of the show, before the singer came on. Jack Eglash, the conductor, was straining his neck to see who was making such a mess of the music. One of the violin players in the front row had his music stand pulled up to cover his face. He was playing wrong notes, playing when he shouldn't be, and generally making a racket. When he was finally singled out, he stopped playing, pushed down his music stand, and the conductor as well as the entire audience saw that it was Jack Benny! Jack put on an expression of being very annoyed at the criticism, and huffed off the stage, leaving the crowd roaring with laughter.

It was very good of him to make such an appearance, giving the audience an extra surprise they would never forget, and bringing more publicity to the show.

Jack invited me to perform in his upcoming farewell television show which was in the planning stages at the time. But he passed away before the program was ever produced, and his death was a sad event for his millions of fans and everyone lucky enough to have known him. Jack Benny was a wonderful, gentle man, and the nicest of the big stars I have ever met in show business.

The I 974 Jerry Lewis Telethon was a great event—not only did it give me the opportunity to meet Jack Benny, but it also exposed me to millions of viewers, as I was fortunate to be one of the artists on the program.

Just before the show, Liberace invited me to a small party he was giving in his suite. He invited me because he had recently heard me sing at the Victor Awards, and had very kindly congratulated me after my performance. I hesitated to attend his little party because I was preparing for my appearance on the telethon, but he personally phoned to once again ask me to come. I'm glad I did, because I enjoyed talking to Liberace very much. We got along well together, and as I was leaving he asked everyone to be quiet and said, "I'd like you all to say good-bye to my good friend, John MacNally from Ireland, who is an absolutely wonderful singer. I want you all to remember his name because you'll hear it plenty in the future."

I thought that was an extremely kind and generous gesture on his part. He was very kind to help me—a virtual unknown to American audiences—feel more confident among the great stars at the telethon.

Following my Las Vegas engagements, I traveled throughout the country to sing at the St. Regis in New York City, the Fairmont in San Francisco, the Crystal Forest Room in Houston, the Diplomat in Miami, the Caribe Hilton in Puerto Rico, and several other beautiful hotels where stars such as Tony Bennett regularly performed .

My shows in the major cities were highlighted by guest appearances on television programs including "The Tonight Show with Johnny Carson" (which was hosted by Barbara Walters on my particular night), "The Mike Douglas Show,' and

"The Merv Griffin Show." I found Merv Griffin to be an exceptionally nice man, and he was very kind to me. It was always exciting to meet these and other famous personalities along the way, such as the actor Telly Savalas, who, when I performed with him in Los Angeles, had not yet reached the great success his "Kojak" series would bring.

In spite of all the work I was getting in the United States, it was a difficult time because I was separated from my family. I couldn't bring two small children on the road, so Anne and the children had returned from Australia to our home in Ireland. It was confusing for Elizabeth and Austin to move again, and to be without their father for such long periods of time. It was terrible to hear little Austin cry over the telephone because he missed me, and at times I regretted the career and the lifestyle it imposed upon me.

As Caruso once said, "The man doesn't have the voice, the voice has the man." These words ring true for every professional singer at some stage in his or her career.

Chapter Six

Australia and Beyond

Shortly after I left the States and joined my family in Ireland, Anne and I decided there was much more opportunity awaiting me in Australia. We left Ireland for the second time and returned to Australia's magnificent eastern seaboard. By an incredible coincidence, the condominium at Bondi Beach was once again for sale, giving us the opportunity to repurchase the lovely place that had been our first Australian home back in 1971.

I was not aware that the Australian government had changed the immigration laws while I was away. We had only been back for three weeks when I got an order to leave the country because I was an illegal alien. Jack Neary came to my aid in this traumatic situation, setting up a meeting with the head of the Immigration Agency, Al Grasby. Mr. Grasby heard me out, was very kind to me, and got me reinstated.

Not long afterward I became a full-fledged Australian citizen at the country's own request, as they wanted me to represent them at the World's Fair in Japan. In the years following I also represented Australia at the World's Fair in Knoxville, Tennessee; New Orleans, Louisiana; and in New York City for the

Australian Bicentennial ceremonies. This gala concert was a sensational event including the great Australian soprano Joan Sutherland, and was held in the Assembly Hall of the United Nations complex.

The incredible success of these international concerts, nationwide tours, and scores of recordings made in Australia from 1975 through the 1980s, proved that our decision to return was a good one.

The story behind receiving my first recording contract in Australia is unique, because it was brought about by the tireless efforts of a very special fan, Hazel Isles. This lovely woman came to nearly all my concerts in Australia, and was determined to get her nephew Brent Currie, an executive of Polygram Records, to hear me. She finally persuaded him to see one of my performances, and after the show he set up a meeting which eventually resulted in a contract. Due to the spunk and tenacity of a fan, I succeeded in getting a contract with this prestigious record label in Australia. I will always be grateful to Hazel Isles.

This contract was the first in a series of remarkably successful recording projects with Polygram Records and CBS Records. I went on to make sixteen albums in Australia, including two platinum albums and four gold albums. One Polygram album's success that was very flattering to me was *Then Sings My Soul*, an album of songs of faith and inspiration. After tremendous sales it went double gold, and was chosen as the official album for the Pope's visit to Australia.

In addition to the new recordings and an exciting concert schedule, one of the more significant events in my life and career took place while I lived in Australia: I quit smoking. Smoking had been a part of my life from about the age of sixteen, when I was a student at Synge Street in Dublin, up until the year 1980. In my youth it didn't have the stigma that it has now. I had given it up many times, sometimes for up to eight and ten weeks at a time, but fell back to the wayside each time. Anne also smoked, but she had given it up in 1975-76, and hadn't smoked since. I knew its dangers, not as much as I know now, but I knew it wasn't good for me. By smoking, a singer is tempting fate and doing his or her best to ruin the God-given gift of the voice. It's amazing the things you'll do to destroy what you love most.

In 1980, Jack Chown, my very close friend in Australia who has been like a father to me in many ways, was really after me to stop smoking. I was beginning to wake up in the morning with a bit of a wheeze in my breathing, and I did notice that when I was doing engagements that required me to sing every night for two or three nights, or maybe twice in the same night, I was having a little problem with hoarseness

Then my brother Donal, his wife Carolyn, and their two youngest, Kevin and Niamh, came to have a holiday with us in Australia, and Donal said, "You really will have to stop smoking, because it's going to affect you in the long run." So we agreed that I would make an effort to stop on a certain date, February 26. It was a very big decision for me, and for weeks before my quitting day I was smoking twice as much as I would normally smoke, in anticipation of giving it up. The week before the day I was to quit, I decided I would give it a trial run for a week. See how smart one can be!—give it a trial run, and when the day of reckoning comes, you say to yourself and everybody else, "Well, I'm not going to really bother, I'm not going to go to the trouble."

One morning, about a week before I was scheduled to give it up, I went to a hypnotherapist. I had heard a lot about it, and I wanted to see if he could do anything for me. I went to this fellow in Bondi Junction, in Sydney. I took a seat in his very nice office, and told him my problem. He asked me how long I'd been smoking, and we decided to have a go with the hypnotherapy. So he asked me to lie down on a couch, put a pair of headphones on my head and said, "Now, I'll be back in a while." So the music started, and his voice began speaking through the headphones. Being a musician and a singer, I'm used to listening to tapes and experiencing the dramatic effects of music, so I followed the music and didn't pay much attention to what he was saying. He wasn't saying anything I didn't already know; he was just stating the obvious ill effects of smoking and so forth. I lay there for what must have been about forty minutes. By the time he came back, I was up to the teeth with listening to him and his music. So I took the headphones off and sat up, and he sat behind his desk. With his slightly arrogant demeanor he made a short statement about the evils of smoke.

I was surprised that he appeared to be pushing me out the door. "Is that it?" I asked.

"Yes," he said. "That's the treatment for today. The reason I use the recording is that if I were to speak to my patients every day, with the length of time I have to speak on the tapes, I'd have no voice left at the end of the week."

I looked at this guy, and thought he was half-mad. And he said, "That will be forty dollars." So I said to him, "You have as much chance now of getting forty dollars off me as a pig has of flying." He got very indignant, saying that that was his professional fee. And I said, "How many of these visits do you require?" So I said, "My friend, if I gave the excuse to my audiences or to the people who book me that if I was to sing every night at every performance I would have no voice at the end of the week, and sent them a tape and a photograph of myself, what effect do you think that would have?"

I gave him twenty dollars and said, "That's twenty dollars too much, but take it and be happy with it." And I got up and walked out. I was so annoyed.

On the way home I started to talk to myself, and tried to psyche myself up. *Since that day I haven't smoked a cigarette.* I haven't even had a pull off of anyone else's. But the effort to do it was very difficult. In fact, I've spoken to doctors who treat addictions of all descriptions, and they say to give up cigarettes is almost as difficult as giving up heroin, and some believe it's even more difficult. For anywhere from four to six weeks, I was awake every morning at about a quarter to three and couldn't go back to sleep. The effect it has on your metabolism is just extraordinary. It also had quite an effect on my voice for about the first three months. I couldn't get rid of the frogs in my throat, and I was coughing up phlegm all the time. I thought my voice would be clear as a bell after giving it up, but in fact it was worse. I found that for the first six or seven months I was more susceptible to colds, sore throats, and so forth. It's difficult to imagine the full effect tar and nicotine have on your body and your mind. Thank God I can say I survived and gave up smoking. There is no doubt in my mind that had I not given up smoking when I did, I would not be singing now as I am. Because I believe I am singing now, at this point in my career, better than I ever have before.

For two years afterward, I'd be at a party, perhaps having a glass of wine, and all of a sudden my hand would be in my pocket for no reason at all. I'd look down, and my hand would be in my pocket searching for something. It was for a packet of cigarettes, of course. So I encourage anybody, particularly anyone in the music business or in the business of singing, to make a supreme effort to give up a habit that destroys everything in your body, particularly your lungs and your breathing.

It is the worst possible thing you can do for your voice. I know many great singers who smoke, great classical singers. It never ceased to amaze me that John McCormack, the great Irish tenor, smoked, and smoked quite heavily. In fact, one of the causes of his death at the premature age of sixty or sixty-one was emphysema. I thank God, every time I see somebody smoking, that he gave me the strength to give it up. You need that strength, an inner strength, to give it up. You also need people who support you, and I definitely had one or two people that were very encouraging. The most encouraging was Anne, of course. She had been through it herself, and was at my side every step of the way.

One of the most important people I met upon my return to Australia was Moira Briody, a great singer and pianist. Moira was born in Longford, Ireland, my mother's hometown, but had lived in Australia for many years. As soon as I discovered what an exceptional musician she was, I asked Moira to be my accompanist, and we performed throughout Australia together.

In addition to the public concerts that gave us our livelihood, Moira and I also performed benefit concerts for various charities. One of the benefits we did every year was for the Matthew Talbot Hostel for homeless men in Sydney. My wife Anne and the other members of the Catholic Women's League in Bondi organized these annual concerts and raised money for this very good cause. The Matthew Talbot Hostel is named after a Dublin man who did wonderful deeds for his fellow Dubliners, particularly homeless men, and who is now in line for sainthood in the Catholic church.

Another great musician I befriended in Australia was Robert Allman, O.B.E., the country's leading operatic baritone. We played a lot of golf together, and had many conversations about singing technique that were a tremendous help to me. It had been decades since my formal training with teachers like Dennis Noble back in Dublin, and all the popular tunes I had been singing and recording took some of the focus away from those early lessons. But Robert helped me regain that knowledge, and taught me that every style of singing—from country and pop to opera—must be done with the correct technical ability if the singer wants to have longevity in the business.

What a godsend to have Robert enter my life at that point in my career! His valuable insights brought about a genuine vocal reawakening in me. Without the correct "placement" of the voice and solid breath control, I wouldn't be able to sing a pop song like "The Wind Beneath My Wings" and then successfully shift gears to perform Schubert's "Ave Maria." Golfing with Robert on the sprawling greens of Australia was not only fun, it was enlightening.

Back in Ireland, my brother Donal was making plans for me. Dublin had a brand-new concert hall which was attracting all the major artists in Europe, both classical and popular. Donal's sharp musical and business senses told him that the time was ripe for a "John MacNally" homecoming concert at the National Concert Hall, and he did a brilliant job making it all happen. I invited Moira to join me and play for the concerts, which would be televised and recorded, and she was thrilled to have the opportunity to return to Ireland and perform in the new hall.

Awaiting me at the Dublin airport was a party of distinguished guests and friends, including Michael O'Halloran, Lord Mayor of Dublin; Christy O'Connor, the great Irish golfer; and Sir Peter Lawler, the Australian ambassador to Ireland and the Vatican. This tremendous homecoming was just the beginning—Donal had arranged for Dr. Patrick Hillery, the President of Ireland, to be the guest of honor for one of the National Concert Hall concerts, and Ambassador Lawler to be the guest of honor on another evening. In his own entrepreneurial way, Donal publicized two of the concerts as the "Presidential night" and the "Ambassadorial night," and had no problem selling advance tickets.

Both in attendance and reception, the National Concert Hall concerts were a phenomenal success. I seem to perform my best for exciting events such as these, when the adrenaline is really flowing and I can feel my nerves. Being a little bit nervous is a good thing for my performance, and I know I'm lucky in that respect because there are many singers whose nervousness locks them up and prevents them from singing at all. There's plenty of time to wind down later, with a good meal and some wine. Depending upon the outcome of the concert and how much energy I've received from the audience, it takes from one to three hours to relax, and it's always nice to have someone to talk to about how things have gone.

The evening President Hillery was in attendance, the concert was broadcast over Irish Television, taped for video release, and a live album recording was made. I now travel to Ireland at least once a year to do concerts at the National Concert Hall, the Cork Opera House, and several other locations. Whenever I am in Ireland, I also try to perform benefit concerts for the Coal Fund, a charity set up to buy coal and fuel for the poor and homeless of Dublin during the winter months. These concerts are traditionally held at the Lord Mayor's mansion in Dublin.

The popularity of the National Concert Hall performances led to a number of television appearances in Ireland. Irish Television even produced a special show documenting my life, the "Bi Bi Show," that brought many of my family and friends together for a lovely night of memories.

Two great friends from our old neighborhood on Templeville Road, Ed and Margaret Hearns, made our homecoming visit much more pleasant and organized than it would have been without their help. They went to great lengths to arrange groups to attend the performances, and were enormously supportive in every way. Every time we return to Ireland, these thoughtful friends can't seem to do enough for us.

Moira and I also did a concert in the cathedral of her hometown, Longford. Driving there from Dublin, we passed through the village of Edgeworthstown, and Moira mentioned that this was the place of her birth. I insisted that we search for her house, and we drove along the unmarked country lanes for quite a while before we stumbled upon the place. I persuaded her to go up to the house, knock on the door, explain who she was, and ask to have a look. It had been thirty-five years since she last saw the house, and she didn't want to bother anyone. But she finally walked up to the door and knocked, and an old man answered. Before she had a chance to open her mouth and introduce herself, the man said, "Hello, Miss Briody." Moira nearly passed out; she couldn't believe anyone would recognize her after all those years. This delightful sidetrack on our way to the cathedral amused Moira for years afterward.

The Irish President, Dr. Patrick Hillery, enjoyed the National Concert Hall performance so much that he bought some of my tapes, and has since told me he enjoys playing them in his car during long journeys in the country. Since meeting President Hillery in 1984, I have had the honor of visiting him many times at the historic presidential residency named Arus an Uachtarain. My love of history has made each visit to this fascinating building a pure delight.

When Dr. Hillery planned his official Australian visit, which was to be the first of its kind for an Irish president in office, he asked me to put on a concert for him and several honorable guests at Sydney Town Hall. My brother Donal and Fred O'Donovan traveled from Ireland to produce this concert, and they brought with them Johnny McCormack, the grandson of the legendary Irish tenor, John McCormack. Moira Briody was my accompanist, and this gala event was attended by President Hillery and all his aides from Ireland; staff from the Australian

Prime Minister's office; Cardinal James Freeman of Sydney, who became a very close family friend; leaders from the Jewish and Protestant faiths; heads of the armed forces; and many others.

Johnny McCormack journeyed to the Sydney concert as a special guest, due to my long involvement in the John McCormack Society. Johnny's father, Cyril, was a good friend who told me inside stories about his famous father. I have given lecture demonstrations on John McCormack and his art, and have found everything about the great singer's life to be a source of fascination and admiration. I once gave a concert at John McCormack's home, Moore Abbey, which since his death had been bought by the Catholic church and used as a home for the mentally handicapped. Before he died, Cyril presented me with his father's magnificent gold jewelry container, a beautiful object with the initials J . M . C . inscribed upon it .

I decided to use the money that was given at the door from the Sydney Town Hall concert to set up a special scholarship fund, the John McCormack Fund, at the Conservatory of Music in Sydney. Young Australian musicians can use these funds when they travel to England and elsewhere in Europe to study with renowned teachers. The first recipient of a scholarship from the John McCormack Fund was Bridget Bolliger, a young flute player whom I invited to play in that Sydney Town Hall concert. It's wonderful to receive letters from students who have used these funds, and to learn how their travels and studies have furthered their young careers. When performing in Ireland, I love to invite winners of the Féis Ceoil to participate in my programs, thereby giving them a bit of exposure to audiences and offering them as much encouragement as I can.

Just as Dublin's National Concert Hall is one of the premier places to perform in Europe, Carnegie Hall is synonymous with

GAY BYRNE

MY WORLD

Sunday World Nov. 1985

NOT only was The Concert Hall full on Saturday week for John MacNally, they had to put the overflow up on the stage with him.

The extra punters nearly found themselves in the choir. Handily enough, there is in the foyer of The Concert Hall a photograph of Count John McCormack in concert somewhere similarly surrounded on stage by fans. So Mr. MacNally is on the tail of a good precedent.

Such overfill is a huge compliment to any artist.

John MacNally had an adoring public on Saturday and he sang his heart out for them. He has a grand manner on stage: relaxed, informal and completely without strain. It's especially heartening to be in a hall which is packed to capacity for one of our own. Not that celebrated foreigners aren't welcome, you understand; but adulation for a fellow you went to school with is nicer.

John MacNally at the N.C.H.

By George Hodnett

TO the National Concert Hall on Wednesday came Dublin-born John MacNally, for a special Millennium concert in which he sang to a gratifyingly filled house. It contained many of his friends who had made the pilgrimage, so that his dedications of songs were many. Our Lady's Choral Society was conducted by Robin Moore, and for items such as "The Holy City" and of course "Molly Malone" the audience were requested to join in.

His voice is indeed a great one, in some points of quality putting one in mind of that of the late Count John McCormack, and this becomes particularly evident in songs from that repertoire, such as "The Irish Emigrant" which was the first song he ever heard sung by McCormack. "The Croppy Boy", again, was a magnificent performance — ideally accompanied, as were all the items, by Russell Ames of whom he remarked, at this point, "He's not Irish — but by the way he plays you can see we're working on it."

Mr Ames did a particularly fine job on "Ireland, Mother Ireland" with its rather unusual (for its period and provenance) construction. The choir's "Finlandia" showed the quality and cohesion for which they are known, and another *tour de force* was Mr MacNally's unaccompanied "Amazing Grace". And as for (virtually compulsory in a visiting artist's programme) "Danny Boy", how nice it is to hear a version that has absolutely nothing wrong with it. Production was by Fred O'Donovan.

from the Chairman

AN CEOLÁRAS NÁISIÚNTA
THE NATIONAL CONCERT HALL

Earlsfort Terrace, Dublin 2, Ireland.
Telephone: Dublin 711888. Telegrams: Ceoláras Dublin.

18 December 1985

Mr. John McNally
Gordon Avenue
Coogee
Sydney
AUSTRALIA

re: Television Spectacular and Concert

Dear John,

Now that you have left the Emerald Isle and returned to your home in Australia I thought I would drop you a line and congratulate you on your success of both the television spectacular and the concert,

It is truly amazing the reaction we have had and since the Concert Hall opened in 1981 we have never had a concert where we actually had to seat the audience on the stage - it was truly remarkable, and is still the talk of Dublin.

Not since the great John McCormack himself played in the Sydney Town Hall where the audience were actually on stage have the people seen anything like your concert.

As a professional producer, myself, I fully appreciated your professionalism and to be able to hold an audience for two hours and then receive a standing ovation and numerous encores in fact I think you could have stayed on stage for another hour.

Once again sincere thanks and as Chairman of the National Concert Hall may I say that you are always welcome.

Warmest personal regards,

Fred O'Donovan

■ THE ARTS
MUSIC REVIEW

Versatile Irish Tenor Warms Up Lincoln Center Crowd

■ Tenor John MacNally

AMY & JOE CARROLL THEATRICAL PRODUCTIONS, INC

What an exhilarating experience to be present when John MacNally, whose estimable tenor voice is recognized in much of Europe and Australia as one of the finest ever to come out of Ireland, befriended New York.

It was a different sort of concert for Lincoln Center—less formal than the usual fare for that venerable performing-arts mecca. There was nearly as much talk as music, and the musical and conversational threads were both integral to the experiential fabric in which MacNally dressed the evening for his audience.

Excerpts from a wash of humor as fluidly good-natured as an Irish cream: "Well, thank you all for coming .... I'm happy you came because it would be a terrible bore here, standing up here singing by myself.... That's what all singers do, you know, whether you like it or not—they sing what they think they sing best, and hope that maybe it's what you wanted to hear, too." And again, en route to a side table for his second drink of water: "Those of you who're wondering what's in the glass—you're right. Comes a shocking silence, you know, when I'm off here getting a drink. So if you could keep the applause going till I'm finished."

There was, of course, more than good humor. There was also splendid singing. In his Lincoln Center debut at Alice Tully Hall, this very astute entertainer not only delivered a virtually flawless performance of two dozen widely varied materials, including some handsomely communicated German lieder and the traditional French "Plaisir d'Amour," but John MacNally also endeared himself to his

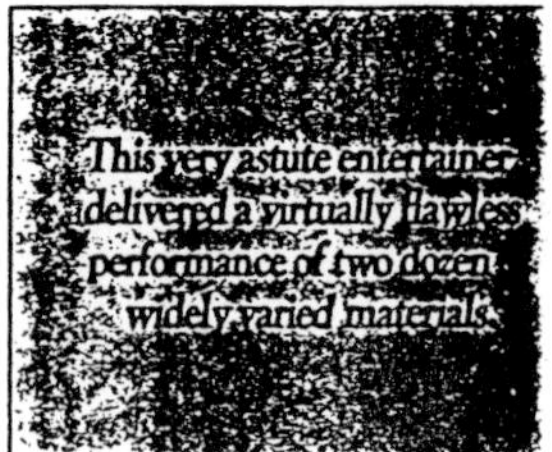

This very astute entertainer delivered a virtually flawless performance of two dozen widely varied materials.

public with the easy grace and sincere humanity that characterize his approach to both his art and his audience.

Typical of both the character and the skill of MacNally's work for the evening was the selection "Little Town in Auld County Down," whose middle-register final tone MacNally lofted up an octave with singular grace and without a trace of self-consciousness.

His is a Mozart-sized voice, well used. One never doubted whether his voice would last through two hours of singing. That is evidence of a well-practiced technique. His fine breath control, moreover, would arouse the envy of any singer.

MacNally, who has sung opera, made a decision early in his professional life to engage in a broader spectrum of styles than are traditionally available to singers who concentrate on classical repertoire. He has appeared extensively in Europe and in his adopted home, Australia, doing just that—very engagingly.

It goes against the grain of some classical traditions that one of the arias performed by MacNally, who is billed as a tenor, was one of the baritone Papageno's arias from Mozart's *Die Zauberflaute,* and I should like to have heard more of his upper register than is demanded by some of the materials he offers. At the same time, his lower register, which is more extensive than expected of men who sing tenor, has a handsome color.

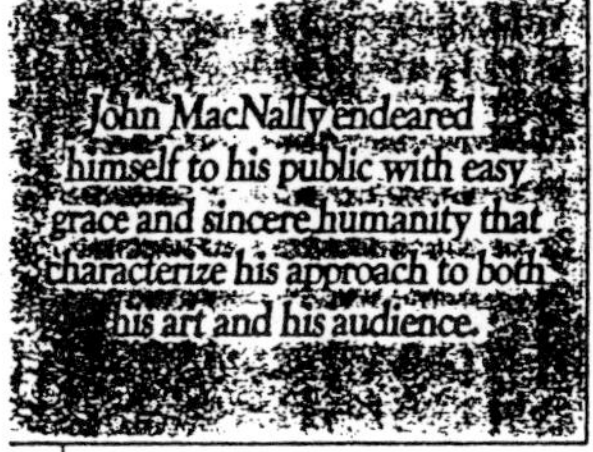
John MacNally endeared himself to his public with easy grace and sincere humanity that characterize his approach to both his art and his audience.

The second half of the program got under way after MacNally, leaning on the piano goodnaturedly as late-returning hearers drifted back to their seats, announced with a grin, "Well, I'm glad you all came back—that's always the crunch, you know." This portion of the evening was similar in tone, though slightly different in character, as MacNally performed requests that he had asked his audience to give to public-relations personnel during the interval.

There was "I'll Take You Home Again, Kathleen," "Maggie," and "Mother Machree," and of course there was "Kathleen Mavourneen."

The content was widely varied and entertaining, and there was something for every taste, though an audience assembled of only classical-music lovers would probably have opted for more operatic material.

I am a classics lover, however, and I was satisfied. It is really a question of taste. *De gustibus* .... All I know for sure is that my own tastes were fully gratified. I guess we were a crowd of honorary Irishmen for the evening, and content to be so.

I don't think I've ever heard a better Schubert's "Ave Maria." Velvet!

MacNally, of course, is as Irish as the "Danny Boy" he sang for one of several encores, and he excels in traditional Irish material, bringing to it an uncommon sensitivity and an authenticity that only a native practitioner of this cultural and musical heritage can impart. It was principally of such materials that his program was assembled. I enjoyed those materials the most, and the color of the voice as it touched them. There were a few husky sounds, but they did not diminish the pleasure of hearing so finely polished a performer.

What is particularly compelling about John MacNally's work is the direct involvement he seems to have with each thing he sings, presenting an emotional scope difficult to describe. Suffice it to say that, if it is possible to be both very earthy and absolutely unearthly at once, MacNally is both as he relates the miracle of "Scarlet Ribbons" with ineffable tenderness, enacts "Old Man River" with tangible pathos, floats a concluding high tone with the most poignant lyricism, or tells an Irish gag with all the ready delight of a kid blowing bubbles.

He is an Irish festival in a tuxedo. Not a complete Irish festival, however. No brawling. What fun. I had a great time. I couldn't thank him enough.

At the end of it all, he thanked his audience for coming, and asked those present not to run away because he'd like to meet them.

They didn't run away and he met them, but only after leading them in each of the several refrains of "Jerusalem," which was his final encore.

A sing-along, no less, at Alice Tully Hall! It isn't done, of course. But it was done on this occasion, and it was delightful.

To say it all as simply as one might, John MacNally didn't just perform at Lincoln Center on the eleventh of September. He graduated Lincoln Center *summa cum laude.*

The whole place was on its feet, and if I had had more feet than the pair I own, I'd have stood on them too.

Congratulations, John MacNally. And you come back, do you hear? At your very next convenience. □

—*Emerson Randolph*

St. Mary's Cathedral
Sydney N.S.W.
Australia 2000

8th January, 1980.

Dear Mr. McNally,

This letter is long overdue but all the involvement of Christmas have interferred with my correspondence.

I am just writing to congratulate you on the dignified way that you compered the Christmas Presentation in the Sydney domain. If I have any complaint it is that you did not sing more often yourself. It is good to see a compere who can combine brightness and dignity.

With every good wish,

I remain,

Yours sincerely in Our Lord,

+ James Card. Freeman

ARCHBISHOP OF SYDNEY.

Mr. J. McNally,
1/54 Fletcher Street,
SOUTH BONDI, N.S.W. 2026

ԱՌԱՋՆՈՐԴՈՒԹԻՒՆ ՀԱՅՈՑ

DIOCESE OF THE ARMENIAN CHURCH OF AMERICA, 630 SECOND AVENUE, NEW YORK, N.Y. 10016-4885 212 686-0710

Archbishop Torkom Manoogian, Primate

May 15, 1989

Mr. John MacNally
c/o Mr. Michael Copeland
33 East 38th Street
New York, NY 10016

Dear Mr. MacNally:

We extend our deep gratitude to you for being with us at the Ecumenical Service in St. Vartan Cathedral yesterday. How moved we were by the beautiful hymns you sang and by your exquisite voice; the Cathedral was filled with its beauty and power. God bless you for so kindly agreeing to share that beauty with us and with Cardinal Willebrands, for it will indeed be one of our most memorable services of worship in St. Vartan's.

May God be with you on your return to Australia and may His Spirit fill you with abiding wisdom and love.

Prayerfully,

Archbishop Torkom Manoogian
Primate

I am delighted, on the occasion of the Gala Concert in honour of the President of Ireland, His Excellency Dr Patrick Hillery, to be able to convey my best wishes to him, to Mrs Hillery, and to all present.

Dr Hillery's visit is unprecedented in Australian history. No other Irish President nor Prime Minister has until now visited Australia, although up to one-third of Australians have some Irish in them.

The Irish have contributed to all areas of Australian culture, particularly to our folk-singing tradition, and it is appropriate that the President of Ireland should be thus welcomed by John MacNally in the Sydney Town Hall.

I wish your evening every success.

The Hon. R. J. L. Hawke, A.C., M.P.
Prime Minister of Australia

great music and entertainment in the United States. In 1986, the Irish comedian Hal Roach invited me to go to New York City and perform the entire second half of his Carnegie Hall program. Hal Roach was especially very popular with Irish people in America, and the enthusiastic response from this audience was astounding. I had been in Australia for so long that I had forgotten the electrifying excitement that can come only from an American audience. The Carnegie Hall concert was actually my second appearance on that great stage. In 1964 the Irish promoter Hugh Hardy sent me and a group of Irish artists to New York City to do a Carnegie Hall concert with Slim Whitman. Slim was a tall man with a high voice who had sold millions of records by that time, and was famous for his recording of "I'll Take You Home Again, Kathleen."

The response to the 1986 Carnegie Hall concert, in which I had an entire solo act after Hal Roach performed in the first half, was so overwhelming that I immediately received several engagements in New York City and the surrounding area. The highlight of these was a concert at Alice Tully Hall in New York's dazzling Lincoln Center.

Between the many concert trips I've taken on behalf of the Australian and Irish governments and those I've arranged on my own, my career has taken me throughout most of the world. I feel fortunate to have made lifetime friends in Australia, Ireland, and the United States, the country where Anne and I currently make our home.

Chapter Seven

All Roads Lead to Nashville

The sensational events in New York City in 1986 gave me a chance to get reacquainted with some of my friends in the United States, including my longest and best friend in the U.S., John Braunschweig. He's an avid music lover with a preference for classical music, and he sings in a glee club in New York. John knows a lot about singers and all kinds of music, and we keep in very close communication. When we're in New York we stay with John and his wife Carole, and they visit us in Nashville.

I was also very happy to meet with two gentlemen who would soon become major influences in my career, Bill Walker and Norm Anderson of BNJ Records.

I first met Bill at the 1982 World's Fair in Knoxville, where I was representing the Australian government with a stellar group of artists including Olivia Newton-John and Peter Allen. Bill had been hired to conduct the orchestra at the Australian pavilion because he was originally from Sydney. We got along very well, and discovered we shared a kindred spirit as lovers of golf (one of nature's strongest binding forces!). Our friendship developed over the years as Bill and his wife made annual Christmas visits to Sydney, where Bill's parents live.

Like most people who hadn't kept up with the changes in country music, I had a lot to learn about Nashville. There's a big distinction now between "country and western" music and "country" music. Country music has branched out into a wide variety of styles that suit many different tastes. Today's country audiences are ready for just about anything, if it's got good lyrics and is performed with an honest approach. Much to my surprise, I've found that country music audiences are even ready for John MacNally.

Through Bill Walker's influence as a major force in the Nashville recording industry, I got appearances on Ralph Emery's "Nashville Now" television program. Bill introduced me to the show's producer, Bill Turner, and I did my first program in 1987. Country-music audiences are very receptive to Irish songs, because the two styles have a lot in common. Some of the great country classics are derived from Irish melodies, and fiddle music and bluegrass are direct descendants of Irish folk music. My first "Nashville Now" performances were well received, and I continue to do the show at least five times a year.

In the 1980s, Polygram Records, with whom I had recorded many albums in Australia, was changing its format to a heavier rock and heavy-metal orientation. On the advice of Bill Walker and Norm Anderson, I negotiated to buy ninety-five of the songs I had recorded with full orchestra from Polygram Records. When Bill and Norm's record company, BNJ Records, advertised these recordings on American television, my career in the United States came to life.

Within a short time we were hard at work creating brand-new albums in the Nashville studio, with multitalented Bill Walker acting as engineer, producer, and composer/arranger. Making regular visits to Nashville to do the television program and recordings, I spent a lot of time with Bill and his wonderful family. Through the tireless efforts of BNJ Records, I got my green card to work in the U.S. in 1989, and Anne and I made a permanent move to Nashville. I have had a fantastic and rewarding relationship with BNJ Records, and have recorded twelve new albums with them.

In June 1992, I started a 5 week engagement at the Cristy Lane Theater in Branson, Missouri. This was the first time I had ever worked in a theater, or in an atmosphere that was 100 percent country. I discovered that the audiences were very receptive to my type of entertainment and of course I was able to give them the close comparisons between the roots of Irish and country music. I was back again in Branson in 1993, and enjoyed the experience just as much as the first time. Described in a July 1992 New York Times article as a "music boomtown", Branson has thirty-four music theaters and two outdoor amphitheaters offering dozens of live country music and variety shows every day. Approximately six million visitors a year flock to this small town to hear their favorite acts in theaters owned by such stars as Glen Campbell, Ray Stevens, Mel Tillis, Willie Nelson, and Andy Williams. My shows at the Cristy Lane Theater have been enormously successful, and my audiences have included people from all over the United States, Canada, and even Ireland and Australia.

I have found many facets of the country-music scene unique in the world of show business. The artists openly praise and support each other, creating a comfortable, friendly, and warm atmosphere very unlike the big-ego situations often found in pop and classical music.

A perfect example of this unselfish country-music attitude is in the story of my first appearance at the Grand Ole Opry. I appeared on the "Nashville Now" show one afternoon, and Minnie Pearl was another guest on the program. After she heard me sing, she invited me to follow her over to the Grand Ole Opry to talk to the host, Roy Acuff, about getting on the show that very evening. She gave up her spot on the program for me, and introduced me to the audience. I sang "Danny Boy" and received a wonderful reception, and Roy asked me to come back and sing "Maggie," one of his favorite songs. Minnie Pearl is a wonderful lady, always ready to help someone, and unstinting in her praise.

Working with Cristy Lane at her theater in Branson, I have always found her to share this selfless, supportive attitude. Well into her own half of the show, after I had sung the first half, she would solicit more praise from the audience for me by saying "Don't you like John MacNally. Isn't he a wonderful singer?" Kindness, friendliness, and support are common in country music, which is truly refreshing.

Between my recording and television work in Nashville, yearly tours to Australia and Ireland, and concerts throughout the U.S. and Canada, my time is well divided on an international scale. Unlike the days when our children were young, Anne now travels everywhere with me, and we enjoy every moment of it.

Of all the places I have seen around the world, my most memorable visit took place on a trip that Anne, Austin, and I took to France in 1988. We visited Lourdes, which was an inspiring and uplifting experience, particularly when we got inside the grotto where Our Lady is reported to have appeared. Even though I thought the commercialism was a bit overdone in the surrounding shops that sold statues, holy water, and all kinds of memorabilia it was an experience I will never forget. This trip also brought back the memory of a funny story about a small relic from Lourdes that Austin had received from my father many years earlier. My father was a very religious man, and had once made a visit to Lourdes. He brought back a holy medal for Austin, and explained to Austin how special it was and that it was very important to never lose it. Austin was a little child at the time, and to make sure he wouldn't lose it, he swallowed it!

Comfort is important when one travels as much as I do, and I am indebted to the fine service I've always received from American Airlines, Qantas, and Aer Lingus, the Irish airline. The people at Aer Lingus have been very kind to me, especially John Bastable in the New York office and Winnie Hayes at Kennedy Airport. I am grateful for all the support this airline has given my career. Another company that has been a lifesaver during my Dublin visits and concerts is Arnott's Men's Outfitters, a clothing company that has provided me with everything I need, and with wonderful service. D. G. Opel of Dublin, owned by Michael Fitzsimons, provides me with a car during all my visits to Ireland, which is also an uncommonly generous show of support and hospitality.

As of this writing in 1992, our family is spread throughout the world, with Austin living in Australia and Elizabeth making her home in Dublin. Elizabeth is pursuing her dream of a radio-broadcasting career and works for Dublin's Radio 98 FM. I am very proud of her determination to find success on her own merits, as she did not choose to reveal she was my daughter when seeking her job at the station.

Austin lives and works in Australia, and is in love with the outdoor life that has built him into a strong swimmer and a great surfer. He also plays a magnificent game of golf, and it's a great joy to play golf with him.

We all get together at least once a year in Australia during my five- to six-week annual tour of that country. With good friends from coast to coast, an established and exciting tour schedule, and plenty of beaches and golf courses, it's the perfect place for the MacNally family to combine business and pleasure.

Chapter Eight

You Can Take the Man Out of Ireland . . .

Whether at home or traveling, I spend as much time as I can playing golf, the game that has been my passion since I first learned to play on the fair greens of Ireland. I would love to have started the game a little earlier in life, and gone on the circuit during the off times in singing. But the music business is totally unpredictable—there's no way the two careers could be managed together. Nevertheless, I always harbored a secret ambition to be a professional golfer. I play quite well, my handicap fluctuates between four and seven, depending on how much I play, and I've played a lot in Australia, Ireland, and of course, here in America.

A very good friend in Ireland, and the greatest golfer Ireland has ever produced, is Christy O'Connor. I've played a lot of golf with Christy and learned a lot from him. When Christy O'Connor came to play the circuit in Australia, he and his charming wife Mary stayed with us. We had a wonderful time with them, and this legendary Irish celebrity absolutely fascinated our children. One day I asked him to give me a couple lessons out on a cricket ground that wasn't being used at that rime of the year. We went out to the grounds, and I began to swing away while Christy told me what I was doing wrong.

Soon we saw a fellow walking towards us from the distance. As he got closer we noticed he had quite a stern look on his face. Christy asked me, "Are you sure you have permission to practice here?" And I said, "Of course I have, don't worry about it." The man marched up to us and said, "Do you realize what you're doing to my cricket pitch?" I had been practicing something over and over to get it right, and in the process had taken chunks out of the ground. Divots and huge clumps of sod were flying all over the place. Fortunately, this man recognized me and also recognized Christy because he was a golf fanatic, so he just moved us a little bit to the left where we wouldn't be actually on the cricket pitch. But Christy nearly had a seizure when he saw this fellow coming over. I have played with Christy quite a bit in Ireland, thorough gentleman and a wonderful golfer.

I play quite a bit wherever I go. I try to travel with my golf clubs. For an entertainer who works at night, golf can be a tremendous release. It's one of those games you must concentrate on completely; otherwise you'll play badly, and to play golf badly is to not really enjoy it. So it's terrific to get out in the fresh air and fill your lungs with it after breathing heavy, smoky air during the evening. That's one great benefit of golf—it gets you out, and gets you walking. I've made many good and promising business associates playing golf, with people such as Bill Walker of BNJ Records, and Robert Allman, the leading operatic baritone in Australia who helped me get back to a healthy singing technique. I've had some very good friends in the golfing profession in Australia, including Ian Baker Finch in his formative years, before he became the great and famous golfer he is today.

I am very happy to be a member of the best golf course in Nashville, the Nashville Golf and Athletic Club, which is owned and operated by my good friend Chuck Whittamore. When I'm not spending time with friends on the golf course, my favorite form of entertainment is having dinner with friends. Anne and I agree that there's nothing better than a wonderful meal served with good wine and great conversation. I love Italian food, especially pasta, and also salads and soup. I try to avoid eating too much meat or heavier foods, because fitness and good health are absolutely essential for a singer. Anne is a marvelous cook, and has a special talent for preparing a traditional dish from the old country, Irish stew. Many restaurants outside Ireland offer their own versions, but they put too many things into it. There's only one way to make the genuine article, pure and simple. I feel it's my duty as an Irishman to share the authentic recipe for Irish stew as made in Ireland, and as Anne makes it, which is fabulous:

Authentic Irish Stew

Ingredients:

4 large, lean lamb chops
2 large onions
4 potatoes
salt and pepper to taste
2 t. mixed herbs
2 cups water

Method: *On the day before you intend serving the stew, you remove all the fat from the chops. Place the chops in a saucepan with the water, simmer gently for one hour, and set aside. The next day, remove any fat which has come to the surface of the water. Add the onions, cut into fourths, and potatoes, cut into* *halves. Add salt and pepper and the herbs. Cover and simmer gently until the onions and potatoes are thoroughly cooked. It is very important to serve Irish stew piping hot. Before serving, sprinkle each serving with finely chopped parsley.*

On a winter evening, when the wind is whistling down the street, this Irish stew will warm the cockles of your heart.

When you finish having that Irish stew, of course, it's always a lovely thing to have an Irish coffee. I did some promotional work for Paddy's Irish Whiskey in Australia, and became quite proficient at making Irish coffee. I feel it's my duty as an Irishman to share the secrets of preparing the perfect cup of Irish coffee:

Fill a stemmed glass three-fourths full with hot coffee. Next, pour in a teaspoon of sugar, brown sugar if available. It's important to stir until the sugar is completely dissolved, because this is what makes the cream float on top. Then add a nip of whiskey (Irish, if possible!). You can use either pouring cream or whipped cream. The traditionalists use pouring cream, poured into the coffee over the back of a teaspoon. If you've made the coffee correctly, the cream will not sink. The magic of the drink is sipping the mixture of hot coffee, whiskey, and blended sugar through the cool cream.

Even more than the traditional food and drink of Ireland, it is my absolute duty as a singing Irishman to share the story behind what is probably Ireland's most famous piece of culture. Wherever and for whomever I sing, my most frequently requested song is the beloved "Danny Boy."

I never grow tired of singing this song. Most people think it's a love song, and it is, but not in the sweetheart-to-sweetheart sense. It's about the love of a father for a son. A man is saying good-bye to his youngest son before the boy goes off to war. His two older sons have already been killed in battle. The father fears that he may die before he ever sees his son again, and asks the boy to kneel and say a prayer at his graveside if he is dead when he returns. "Danny Boy" is a rare and moving song that never loses its luster for me. I don't know how many times or in how many places I've sung it, but it never fails to touch me or those who hear it. I close my story with the words to this beautiful piece which has had an impact on people all over the world, and on me, throughout my life of song.

Danny Boy

Oh, Danny boy, the pipes, the pipes are calling.
From glen to glen and down the mountain side,
The summer's gone and all the roses falling,
'Tis you 'tis you must go and I must bide,
But come ye back when summer's in the meadow,
Or when the valley's hushed and white with snow.
'Tis I'll be here in sunshine or in shadow,
Oh Danny boy, Oh Danny boy I love you so.

And when ye come and all the flowers are dying
If I am dead as dead I well may be
Ye'll come and find the place where I am lying
And kneel and say an Ave there for me;
And I shall hear though soft your tread above me,
And all my grave shall warmer, sweeter be,
For you will bend and tell me that you love me
And I will sleep in peace, until you come to me.

Discography

• All albums unless otherwise indicated •

Abide With Me
An Evening With John MacNally
Australian Trilogy
Before You Go
Before You Go (*single*)
Desert Song
Don't Let Life Get You Down (*single*)
Evergreen
Evergreen Vol. 1 *
Evergreen Vol. 2*
Evergreen Video* *(10 songs filmed in Australia)*
Favorite Songs Of Love*
For Love Of Ireland*
40 Shades Of Green
From The Heart*
Have You Tried Love
I Still Believe In Love
Ireland' s John MacNally Vol. 1 *
Ireland's John MacNally Vol. 2*
John MacNally Collection
John MacNally Sings Danny Boy & Other Favorites
John MacNally's Christmas*
John MacNally's Ireland
Just For You

Live In Concert*
Live In Concert (With Piano)*
Live In Concert Video*
Lots Of Love
Love And Roses*
Love Songs
Mary In The Morning
Mary In The Morning (*single*)
Mother Machree (*single*)
Naughty Marietta
Picking Up Pebbles (*single*)
Reflections Of Ireland**
Sincerely
Songs Of Faith
Songs Of Ireland
Songs Of Peace And Love
That' s What Friends Are For
The Tenor Of Ireland**
Then Sings My Soul
Then Sings My Soul Vol. 1 *
Then Sings My Soul Vol. 2*

*Most recent releases. **Available in stores throughout America.

* * * * *

Readers wishing to contact John MacNally or join the John MacNally Fan Club may write to:

John MacNally Fan Club
PO Box 5005
Brentwood, Tennessee 37027
U .S .A.